Impeachment

IMPEACHMENT

A Handbook
New Edition

CHARLES L. BLACK, JR.

PHILIP BOBBITT

Yale UNIVERSITY PRESS/NEW HAVEN & LONDON

Yale University Press books may be purchased in quantity for educational, business, or
promotional use. For information, please e-mail sales.press@yale.edu (U.S. office) or
sales@yaleup.co.uk (U.K. office).

Set in Minion type by Newgen North America.
Printed in the United States of America.

Library of Congress Control Number: 2018943233
ISBN 978-0-300-23826-6 (paperback : alk. paper)

A catalogue record for this book is available from the British Library.

This paper meets the requirements of ANSI/NISO Z39.48-1992 (Permanence of Paper).

10 9 8 7 6 5 4 3 2 1

To my sister,
Betty Black Hatchett
With much love
—C.L.B., Jr.

To Pasha and Rebekah
For unto whomsoever much is given, of them shall be
much required; and from those who have been entrusted
with much, much more will be asked.
—P.C.B.

Contents

Preface to the New Edition

It is said that in the United States, a "new & improved" label will always increase sales. This is doubtless a testament to our irrepressible optimism.

Since the publication of *Impeachment: A Handbook,* by Charles L. Black, Jr., in 1974, it has become the standard work. *Lawfare* called it "the most important book ever written on presidential impeachment." Its sales peak whenever there is impeachment talk in the Congress, and staffers can be seen like schoolchildren carrying their *vade mecums.*

As the 2018 midterm elections approached, there was some anxiety—and no doubt, in some quarters, hope—that impeachment might again be undertaken. As it happened, I was teaching the *Handbook* in my Legal Methods class at Columbia as an exquisite demonstration of the forms of constitutional argument. My students complained that the book had been published before any definitive action was taken to remove President Nixon, and they chafed to know how Black would have dealt with the significant questions of the hour—both then and now. Was the hacking of the Democratic campaign chairman's emails in 2016 like the burglary of the Democratic campaign chairman's correspondence at the Watergate complex in 1972? Was the Republican campaign's contacts with Russian diplomats in 2016 like the Nixon campaign's contacts with South Vietnamese diplomats in 1968? Do the House Judiciary Committee's charges against Nixon set a precedent defining an "impeachable offense" arising from improper use of the Justice Department, even though the president resigned before the House could vote on this charge? Was the Clinton impeachment charge for the obstruction of justice a precedent because it was adopted by the House—or not, because the Senate did not convict on this charge? And what about issues Black didn't address, like the relation between the Twenty-Fifth Amendment and impeachment, or the role of the Emoluments Clause as a possible basis for impeachment? And what about the president's pardon power? Are there circumstances in which the issuance of a pardon—or the promise of one—can provide a ground for impeachment?

To all of these questions, I gave the same answer: my students had all they needed in Black's book. It wouldn't tell them *what* to think of these or any other problems, even in the Nixon case, which was unfolding as the book was written. The *Handbook* would instruct them *how* to think. It laid out clearly and concisely the methods by which a legal answer could be derived from the text, history, structure, doctrine, practicality, and ethos of the Constitution, and it showed rather elegantly how to apply these six fundamental methods.

Still, I took the students' point. Black's chapter "Application to Particular Problems" cried out for the application of his methods to the problems raised by the class. And there were important precedents—cases of attempted and partly successful impeachments that created or affirmed doctrine—that had occurred since the book's publication.

Moreover, while Black's masterpiece remained the standard reference work, new books on presidential impeachment were appearing by writers I liked and respected that, because of their intrinsic merit and also because of the consumer bias for the "new & improved," might eclipse the *Handbook* in the marketplace. That would be a great shame, not because there is anything wrong with these new books but because outside the esoteric topic of impeachment, Black's book was a key exposition of how we go about resolving constitutional questions in the absence of a Supreme Court opinion. (This remains, I hate to say, a continuing problem for the field. When asked whether a president could pardon himself, a prominent law professor replied, "There really is no answer to this question since it has never arisen.") Allowing Black's book to gather dust on the library shelves would be far more than simply a loss for the literature on impeachment, which in any case would build on his insights. It would remove a foundation stone from the intellectual edifice that is perhaps the most important advance made in constitutional law during my lifetime: the development of what might be called the "standard model" that enables legislators, citizens, and journalists as well as judges to resolve constitutional questions when there is no authoritative judicial precedent, and to assess judicial opinions when there is a precedent. Black's tour de force is as important to this development as Weinberg and Salam's equations are to the Standard Model in physics.

The one thing I refused to do in this new edition was to touch a word of Black's inimitable writing. It was enough that I was foolishly prepared to put my own stolid texts next to his poet-perfect prose. I would not "revise" Black's work of genius.

So here it is: new (in some respects) but not improved.

Philip Bobbitt
March 18, 2018

Preface

My thanks go to Chester Kerr and to all at the Yale University Press, for extraordinary help and cooperation—but most especially to Jane Isay, the best of editors; to Margaret Abelson, for expert and most timely typing help; to Eileen Quinn, both for that and for valuable suggestions on the manuscript; to the staff of the Yale Law School Library; to Barbara Aronstein Black, for ideas developed in many discussions while the book was germinating, and for several crucial suggestions toward the end. On all public law matters, as in so many other ways, I have benefitted through the years from the works and friendship of Max Gluckman, whose constitutional studies of the Barotse, and of other societies remote from our own, have concentrated in great part on the eternal problems of removal and succession; luckily, he and Mary Gluckman have been in New Haven while this book was being written. I never can publish anything in constitutional law without acknowledging afresh my pervasive debt to Alexander Bickel, for what are now eighteen years of generously given access to his rich store of knowledge and thought.

Vade libelle!

C.L.B., Jr.
New Haven
May 21, 1974

PART I

Charles L. Black, Jr.

CHAPTER 1

Introduction

For the first time in more than a century, and for the second time in our history, the country has in 1974 been faced with the live possibility that a president may, in the words of the Constitution, "be removed from Office on Impeachment for, and Conviction of, Treason, Bribery, or other high Crimes and Misdemeanors."

The presidency is a prime symbol of our national unity. The election of the president (with his alternate, the vice-president) is the only political act that we perform together as a nation; voting in the presidential election is certainly the political choice most significant to the American people, and most closely attended to by them. No matter, then, can be of higher political importance than our considering whether, in any given instance, this act of choice is to be undone, and the chosen president dismissed from office in disgrace. Everyone must shrink from this most drastic of measures.

Yet the Framers of our Constitution very clearly envisaged the occasional necessity of this awful step, and laid down a procedure and standards for its being taken. Their actions on this matter were, as the records of their debates show, very carefully considered. As is true, however, of most other parts of their Constitution, they put in place only a very general framework, leaving it to the future to fill in details, and leaving many questions open to honest difference of opinion. This book is about the procedure and standards set up by the Constitution, and about some of the questions that must still be answered. While all civil officers of the United States, including federal judges, may be impeached, this book centers on presidential impeachment.

When one is writing, as an academic constitutional lawyer, for laymen, on debatable questions of law, one ought perhaps to confess one's biases, so that allowance may be made for these. I should say first that, both in voting and in published writing, I have from my youth quite consistently opposed the president who has been the subject of recent proceedings—except for my having taken the public position, at an early stage in the deplorable train of events leading to those proceedings, that he (or any president) ought to be held to enjoy an ample privilege of confidentiality as to communications with his own staff in the White House, and that, to put it concretely, he was under no obligation to give up the celebrated tapes—a position that enjoyed little support from others. To countervail (as I hope) my lifelong political set against just about all of this president's positions, I confess to a very strong sense of the dreadfulness of the step of removal, of the deep wounding such a step must inflict on the country, and thus approach it as one would approach high-risk major surgery, to be resorted to only when the rightness of diagnosis and treatment is sure.

The Framers of the Constitution have left us, as they must, a legacy not only of certainties but of questions. Where the answer to one of these questions seems to me clear, I shall state and endeavor to support my own position, sometimes trying to state also the arguments for the contrary view. Where, as must often be true, I look on a question as more or less open, I shall so treat it, trying to give arguments on both sides. An understanding of the questions is more important than a fixed conviction concerning the answers.

This book is for the citizen. What part ought the citizen to play in the process of impeachment and removal? My own answer would be that, for the most part, our attitude as to any impeachment ought to be that of vigilant waiting. The impeachment process, whether "judicial," "nonjudicial," "criminal," or "noncriminal," resembles the judicial criminal procedure in that it is confided by the Constitution to responsible tribunals—the House of Representatives and the Senate—and in that these bodies are duty-bound to act on their own views of the law and the facts, as free as may be of partisan political motives and pressures. In this process, a snow of telegrams ought to play no part.

At the same time we cannot, and perhaps ought not try to, keep ourselves free of opinions concerning the process; such views inevitably form themselves as one tries to follow and understand what is going on. In their formation, we ought to try to take the same stance of principled political neutrality that we hope to see taken by the House and the Senate as they go about their work. This is not easy, particularly as to questions that have no certain answers; it is always tempting to resolve such questions in favor of the immediate political result that is palatable to us, for one never can definitely be proved wrong, and so one is free to allow one's prejudices to assume the guise of reason. The best way to combat this tendency is to ask ourselves whether we would have answered the same question the same way if it came up with respect to a president toward whom we felt oppositely from the way we feel toward the president threatened with removal.

One further point: it is the cardinal principle at least of American constitutional interpretation that the Constitution is to be interpreted so as to be workable and reasonable. This principle does not collide with respect for the "intent of the Framers," because their transcendent intent was to build just such a Constitution. American constitutional law, as expounded by judges and others, is full of instances of the application of this principle. Applying it to doubtful questions regarding impeachment, in this book for the laity, I shall give chief emphasis to arguments of a practical cast. Such arguments do not have the fine savor of ancient learning, but they are the ones that usually do prevail in our constitutional law, particularly when it is at its admired best; and they have the advantage that laymen can understand them—in itself not an inconsiderable merit when one is dealing with a constitution meant for all.

For those who wish to pursue any aspect of the subject further, the Bibliography opens every road. The constitutional provisions relevant to impeachment and referred to in the text are gathered in an Appendix.

CHAPTER 2

The Procedures

General

The procedures of the House of Representatives and of the Senate are highly technical, but most of this technicality is irrelevant to essential understanding. Let us consider in broad outline the processes of impeachment and removal.

Strictly speaking, "impeachment" means "accusation" or "charge." The House of Representatives has, under the Constitution, the "sole Power of Impeachment"—that is to say, the power to bring *charges* of the commission of one or more impeachable offenses. These charges are conventionally called "Articles of Impeachment." The House "impeaches" by simple majority vote of those present.

The Senate "tries" all impeachments—it determines, on evidence presented, whether the charge in each Article of Impeachment is true, and whether, if the charge is true, the acts that are proven constitute an impeachable offense. Such an affirmative finding is called a "conviction" on the Article of Impeachment being voted upon. A two-thirds majority of the senators present is necessary for conviction.

This two-stage procedure was borrowed from the British model (impeachment by the House of Commons and trial and conviction by the House of Lords). It is also analogous, obviously, to the two stages in traditional English and American criminal law— "indictment" (or charge) by the grand jury, and "trial" by another jury. The "Articles of Impeachment" correspond to the *counts* in an indictment presented by a grand jury. The Senate's vote on individual Articles, one by one, corresponds to the trial jury's separate verdict on each count of an indictment. This two-stage procedure has obvious merits, in criminal practice and in impeachments. It assures consideration of the evidence by more than one body, and screens out (at the first stage) insubstantial or clearly unprovable accusations, so that the public and private trouble and expense of a full trial are avoided, in all instances where the first or "charging" body—in the case of impeachment, the House of Representatives— finds nothing worthy of full-dress treatment.

The Part of the House of Representatives

Let us now take a more detailed look at procedure in the House of Representatives. Although the Constitution does not require it, the House has always employed one of its committees (usually the Judiciary Committee) to investigate and report on charges that might lead to impeachment; in the presidential case in our times, several resolutions seeking impeachment were referred to the Judiciary Committee for full investigation and recommendation. In only one instance in our history has impeachment ever been voted by the House of Representatives without an affirmative committee recommendation.

The committee to which this task is confided must hear evidence—great masses of it in a complicated case. At this stage it seems certain that no technical "rules of evidence" apply. (Indeed, I shall argue later that they do not apply even in the Senate trial.) Evidence may come from investigations by committee staff, from grand jury matter made available to the committee, or from any other source. Testimony before the committee, and the production of documents or other objects, may be compelled by subpoena—which is an order for appearance, or production, under the threat of criminal penalty. In addition to evidentiary matters, the committee must also consider whether the acts shown probably to have been committed are "impeachable" within the meaning of the constitutional text (of which much more will be said in Chapter 3). What part is to be played at this stage by lawyers of the person under investigation would seem to rest in the sound discretion of the committee. Where the committee concludes, on the facts and on the law, that one or more impeachable offenses are shown with sufficient clarity to justify trial, the committee reports, to the full House of Representatives, its recommendation that one or more "Articles of Impeachment" be adopted.

When this recommendation reaches the full House, it might conceivably be amended, but this is politically unlikely. It is just possible that the House might vote to *drop* one or more Articles of Impeachment, but next to impossible that any would be added, because an Article added against the recommendation of the committee that had heard all the evidence would stand on dubious ground in the Senate and in the country. The House will almost certainly not hear any more evidence but will vote, after debate, on the question whether to impeach or not, voting on all Articles of Impeachment together or on each separately. As a variation on this procedure, the committee may generally recommend impeachment, and if the House votes to follow this recommendation, the matter would be referred back to the committee, for the drafting of Articles; these would then have to be voted on by the whole House.

An affirmative vote by the House sends the Bill of Impeachment, with one or more Articles, to the Senate for trial—just as a grand jury indictment, with one or more "counts," goes to the trial court and jury, for final determination of guilt or innocence.

A majority of the House of Representatives (218 members out of the 435) constitutes a "quorum," so that, with a majority present, business can be transacted. Since a vote of impeachment is by simple majority of those present, Articles of Impeachment might theoretically be voted by one-fourth plus one of the full membership. In fact, it is unlikely that many members would ever absent themselves from the vote on a presidential impeachment. Such an absence would be hard to explain to constituents.

One thing that both the committee and the House leadership will try to avoid is a close vote along party lines—a vote whereby Republicans and Democrats divide as such. An impeachment voted that way would go to the Senate tainted, or at least suspicious, and would be unlikely to satisfy the country, because party motives would be suspected. This desire for bipartisan backing will expectably result in there existing some leverage on the part of the minority members of the committee and of the House—in our times the Republican members. In other words, some compromise will be sought which can win the adherence of at least a fair number of them.

The final role of the House of Representatives is to appoint "managers" to present in the Senate the case for conviction and removal on the Articles of Impeachment. The House, in effect, is the prosecuting party at the Senate trial, and the managers are the House's counsel.

Managers may be chosen either by general ballot on names in the House of Representatives, by passage of a resolution containing a complete list of names, or by a House-passed authorization to the Speaker of the House (its presiding officer) to appoint managers. These managers are congressmen, but they will be assisted by staff—probably drawn from Judiciary Committee staff. Generally, both political parties are represented, but no one would (for obvious reasons) be likely to be made a manager who had not supported the impeachment resolution.

The Part of the Senate

Upon receipt of Articles of Impeachment voted by the House, the Senate must resolve itself into a tribunal for trial. Where the president is accused, the chief justice of the United States presides; in this case, as in the trial of all impeachments, the senators take a special oath (over and above their oaths of office) to "do impartial justice according to the Constitution and laws." Both these circumstances give emphasis to the fact that the Senate—whether for this occasion you call it a "judicial" body or not—is taking on quite a different role from its normal legislative one.

Many other factors, indeed, lead to the conclusion that the Senate's function in impeachments is to be seen as much like that of a judicial court; whether it really "is" such a court is a sterile question of nomenclature. Until a very late stage in the Constitutional Convention of 1787, all drafts of the Constitution provided for trial of impeachments by the Supreme Court; when this was changed to trial by the Senate, there was no hint of any changed conception as to the *nature* of the function or, much more importantly, as to the proprieties of its exercise. The Constitution says, in Article III (the Judiciary Article), that "the trial of all Crimes, except in Cases of Impeachment, shall be by Jury . . ."; the implication is that the impeachment trial is a "trial" much like others, except that a jury is not to be used. The special oath which senators take has already been mentioned. The Senate is to "try" all impeachments, not simply vote on them; the word "try" is a word used almost invariably in regard to judicial trials. Political good sense points the same way; a judicial or quasi-judicial trial is simply one that inquires into the facts and the law, without partisan or narrow political bias, and proceeds to judgment accordingly—these things are obviously what we want in impeachment proceedings. In function, then, the "trial" in the Senate is, as its name implies, at least quasi-judicial. The important thing is not the name given but the thing desired—total impartiality, at least resembling that of a faithful judge or juror.

Here a difficulty arises—one which can be solved only by great and self-insightful integrity. It must almost always be the case that many senators find themselves either definitely friendly or definitely inimical to the president. In an ordinary judicial trial, persons in such a position would of course be disqualified to act, whether as judges or as jurors. It cannot have been the intention of the Framers that this rule apply in impeachments, for its application would be absurd; a great many senators would inevitably be disqualified by it, and it might easily happen that trial would be by a quite small remnant of the Senate. The remedy has to be in the conscience of each senator, who ought to realize the danger and try as far as possible to divest himself of all prejudice. I see no reason why this cannot produce a satisfactory result.

Members of the House of Representatives ought also, in acting on impeachment, to try for the impartiality of a good grand jury member; I have reserved the point to the Senate stage because it is a more critical and crucial one when the final trial is at hand.

On special oath, then, and under the chief justice as presiding officer, the Senate begins to hear evidence on each of the Articles of Impeachment. The case for conviction will be presented by the managers for the House of Representatives; the president will be represented by counsel, but may appear in person, as does the defendant at a criminal trial, though this may be dispensed with by the Senate at the president's request.

Each side will call witnesses and introduce documentary evidence, bearing on the issues framed by the Articles of Impeachment. On any procedural question, including admissibility of evidence, the chief justice will make a ruling, but that ruling may be reversed by a majority vote of the senators present. After all evidence is in, argument will take place.

The Standing Rules of the Senate provide that there may be appointed a "Committee of Twelve" to hear evidence in the trial of impeachment and to report to the full Senate; "twelve" must be borrowed from the jury system. This provision is of dubious constitutionality, in view of the language confiding to "the Senate," and not to some part of the Senate, the "sole Power to try all Impeachments." It seems unlikely that such a procedure would be followed in the trial of a president, where it is essential that absolute bedrock legitimacy be inarguably present—and where the business of the trial is the most important business, by far, to which any senator could be attending.

After all evidence and argument have been heard, the Senate must vote. The vote is separate on each Article of Impeachment. If no Article registers a two-thirds vote for conviction, a judgment of acquittal is pronounced and recorded. If one or more Articles of Impeachment receive a vote of two-thirds or more, then the president is convicted, and judgment of conviction and removal is pronounced by the chief justice.

The Constitution says that the impeached officer "shall be removed" on conviction of "Treason, Bribery, or other high Crimes or Misdemeanors." There may be a question whether this language is absolutely mandatory, with no possibility of distinctly lesser action, such as reprimand. It may be that some power of mercy or leniency is to be read into any such language by implication, unless expressly excluded. But the question is not at all likely to arise in a presidential case; if there were a disposition to leniency, this disposition would almost certainly take the form of an aborting of the process at a much earlier stage. Politically, the country could not live with a president actually convicted of "Treason, Bribery, or other high Crimes and Misdemeanors." It seems to be optional with the Senate whether to impose the additional penalty of disqualification from office. No "further" punishment of any kind may be imposed, though the removed officer, including an ex-president, may later be tried and punished in the ordinary courts, for the very offenses that were grounds of removal.

In voting on each Article of Impeachment, each senator, acting in a capacity combining those of judge and jury, is registering his best judgment "on the facts" and "on the law." This means that he is answering two questions together: "Did the president do what he is charged in this Article with having done?" "If he did, did that action constitute an impeachable offense within the meaning of the constitutional phrase?"

It might be emphasized, finally, that the senator's role is solely one of acting on the accusations (Articles of Impeachment) voted by the House of Representatives. The Senate cannot lawfully find the president guilty of something not charged by the House, any more than a trial jury can find a defendant guilty of something not charged in the indictment. This follows from elementary principles of fair notice, as well as from the linkage implied by the constitutional phrase, ". . . on Impeachment for, and Conviction of . . ." It could hardly make sense to read this as allowing impeachment for one thing and conviction for another. As an obvious corollary, Senate acquittal is not an endorsement of the president, or even an approval of his conduct, but only establishes that the senators voting in the negative were unconvinced of his guilt on the actual Articles of Impeachment brought in by the House of Representatives.

Of course, any material uncovered in the course of a Senate trial might be matter for a new impeachment in the House of Representatives. But the cumbersomeness of this, as well as its political un-likelihood, makes it highly desirable that the House be very careful to draw its Articles so as to charge offenses that can be proved, and that are likely to be held impeachable by the Senate.

Some Special Procedural Points

IS IMPEACHMENT, WITH TRIAL THEREON,
A "CRIMINAL PROCEEDING"?

The president is impeachable for "Treason, Bribery, and other high Crimes and Misdemeanors." Treason is a crime. Bribery is a crime. It would seem that a "high Crime" must in some sense be a crime. What about a "misdemeanor" or "high misdemeanor"? It seems unlikely that such a phrase, in such a string, abruptly changes the subject. Nevertheless, some have contended that impeachment, and Senate trial, are not criminal proceedings at all.

The best thing to say about this question is that it need never have been asked in general form. It makes no difference whether we *call* impeachment a "criminal" proceeding or not, any more than it makes any difference whether we *call* it a "judicial" proceeding or not. What does make a difference is ascertaining those things in the impeachment process that should be treated *like* the same things in a criminal trial, and what things need not be. On this question, or set of questions, much can usefully be said.

Let us take first the question of proper attitude toward the *facts,* and toward the problems of *proof,* and of *burden of proof.* As a simple, and typical, factual question, let us take, "Did the president, on a given day, and at a given time, say 'X' or 'Y'?"

Now in a civil, noncriminal trial, say, an automobile accident case, if some witnesses testify that "X" was said, and others testify that "Y" was said, the juryman or judge must decide whom to believe, and if he finds slightly more credible the testimony of the "X" witnesses, he "finds" that "X" was said. The usual noncriminal rule is that the facts are determined by mere "preponderance of the evidence," as that preponderance registers with the judge or jury.

In a criminal case, on the other hand, guilt must be established "beyond a reasonable doubt." In the example I have given, if there were no very clear or cogent reason for believing one witness or set of witnesses over another, the duty of the trier of fact would probably be to find for the defendant, since mere conflicting testimony, with no clearcut and weighty reason for believing either side, creates a doubt that cannot usually be said to be "unreasonable."

Of course the example I have given is almost unrealistically simple. A more realistic issue of fact might be, for example: "Did the official on trial perform an action *because* a campaign contribution was given, or was this a coincidence?" Either is possible; the "finding" of this "fact"—the "fact" of corrupt or blameless motivation—may entail the drawing of complicated inferences from circumstances; the circumstances themselves may be proven with more or less clarity. Before the "fact" can be "found," the trier of fact must decide on a standard of proof. Should he find an impeached president guilty of corruption if it seems slightly more likely than not that a corrupt motive was present? Or should a finding of guilt have to rest, as in a criminal trial, on evidence which leaves no "reasonable doubt"? It makes a big difference, as the example I have just given shows.

Nor is the matter quite this simple, for there are intermediate rules in between the "mere preponderance" rule and the "reasonable doubt" rule. As to some questions in some civil cases, for example, "clear and convincing" evidence is required—something *more* than a mere 51% "preponderance" of evidence, but something *less* than evidence leaving no room for reasonable doubt. What is the right standard for judging guilt in an impeachment proceeding?

Of course we don't know the answer with any sureness; we have to work it out for ourselves. As with so many constitutional questions, we have to ask what is reasonable, and the reply is here far from obvious. Removal by conviction on impeachment is a stunning penalty, the ruin of a life. Even more important, it unseats the person the people have deliberately chosen for the office. The adoption of a lenient standard of proof could mean that this punishment, and this frustration of popular will, could occur even though substantial doubt of guilt remained. On the other hand, the high "criminal" standard of proof could mean, in practice, that a man could remain president whom every member of the Senate believed to be guilty of corruption, just because his guilt was not shown "beyond a reasonable doubt." Neither result is good; law is often like that.

Of course each senator must find his own standard in his own conscience, as advised by reflection. The essential thing is that no part whatever be played by the natural human tendency to think the worst of a person of whom one generally disapproves, and the verbalization of a high standard of proof may serve as a constant reminder of this. Weighing the factors, I would be sure that one ought not to be satisfied, or anything near satisfied, with the mere "preponderance" of an ordinary civil trial, but perhaps must be satisfied with something a little less than the "beyond reasonable doubt" standard of the ordinary criminal trial, in the full literal meaning of that standard. "Overwhelming preponderance of the evidence" comes perhaps as close as present legal language can to denoting the desired standard. A unique rule, not yet named by law, may find itself, in the terrible seriousness of a great case. Senators have no plainly authoritative guide in this matter, and ought not to be censured for the rule they conscientiously choose to act upon, after thought and counsel, and above all in total awareness of the dangers of partisanship or feelings of distaste.

Another question, concealed by the question whether impeachment is a "criminal" matter—or even a judicial matter—is "What rules as to the admissibility of evidence ought to be enforced?" In an ordinary trial, for example, we exclude what we call "hearsay" evidence—testimony by one witness that another person, not a witness, told the witness that something had happened. We exclude evidence of the defendant's character, unless he himself seeks affirmatively to establish his good character. And so on through a considerable range of technicality.

Here, I think, the sensible answer comes clear. These technical rules of evidence were elaborated primarily to hold *juries* within narrow limits. They have no place in the impeachment process. Both the House and the Senate ought to hear and consider *all* evidence which seems relevant, without regard to technical rules. Senators are in any case continually exposed to "hearsay" evidence; they cannot be sequestered and kept away from newspapers, like a jury. If they cannot be trusted to weigh evidence, appropriately discounting for all the factors of unreliability that have led to our keeping some evidence away from juries, then they are not in any way up to the job, and "rules of evidence" will not help.

A third question concealed in the question whether impeachment is "criminal" has to do with the *law*. It is a cardinal principle of Western justice that criminal punishment ought not to be visited on anyone without clear warning of the criminality of his acts. It cannot be said that the phrase "high Crimes and Misdemeanors" has the clarity we would require of an ordinary criminal statute. Yet it is the phrase the Framers gave us; in the next chapter we will try to resolve some of the issues concerning it, though not all are tractable to resolution. At this stage, perhaps, all we can say is that a conscientious senator ought to insist upon being quite clearly convinced that the impeached official knew or should have known the charged act was wrong, before he votes for conviction. This simple rule should resolve many difficulties.

SHOULD HEARINGS BE PUBLIC?

There may be early stages in the investigation process in the House when confidentiality should be maintained. Public disclosure of raw evidence, not yet evaluated as to credibility or relevance, might do some harm, and can do no good. In the later stages, and certainly in the Senate trial, it seems to me that the proceedings should be just as open as those in any courtroom. With reporters present, and with members of the public coming and going in the galleries, all danger of substantial secrecy would vanish. Trial on an impeachment is public business.

I would on the other hand (though I am certain that others will disagree) most strenuously advocate that radio, television, and cameras have no more place in this solemn business than they have in any other trial, and for the same reasons. There is no point in inflicting humiliation greater than that inflicted by the mere fact of impeachment. Nothing solid is added to public information by making a continuing spectacle of a trial. Above all, television, radio, and photography *act* upon that which they purport to *observe*; what one sees and hears is not what would have occurred if these modern means of communication were not there. At least there is a great danger of this, a danger often realized in the past, and that is enough to justify exclusion.

Continual nationwide television exposure contains another danger: it maximizes the chances of development of public pressure for some given result. It is of course the duty of senators not to take such pressure into account, but we would regard as totally unfair any other sort of trial where such pressure was applied. It therefore seems wrong to encourage it. The judgment of the public ought to come after the fact, on sober and long consideration of a record which will remain accessible forever. Play-by-play coverage contributes in no way to the formation of this ultimate evaluation, the only one that counts. The taking, at intervals, of public opinion polls on guilt or innocence, should be looked on as an unspeakable indecency.

IS THERE ANY "PRESIDENTIAL PRIVILEGE" IN IMPEACHMENT PROCEEDINGS?

Early in the investigations leading to the commencement of the latest presidential impeachment process, the president claimed the privilege of withholding from other branches of government the tenor and content of his own conversations with his close advisers in the White House. I regarded this claim as moderate and reasonable, and thought its upholding was essential to the efficacious and dignified conduct of the presidency and to the free flow of candid advice to the president. There was little public agreement with the view I then expressed, and the lower courts, though granting some scope to the privilege, took a very narrow view of it. I hope the question can be reconsidered in quieter days; I do not desire to unsay anything I have said. As time went on, however, the factual situation changed. The president himself released copious quantities of what I would have regarded as privileged material. Further, the issue, for purposes of the impeachment process, is not whether any federal or state court, or any committee of Congress, can force revelation of the president's conversations with his close advisers, but whether that can lawfully be done by a House committee conducting an impeachment investigation, or by the Senate at an impeachment trial.

As to the effect of the release of some material by the president, I wholly reject the theory that the president "waives" his privilege of confidentiality by releasing some material as to which the privilege might have been claimed. The enforcement of this "waiver" seems to me wholly wrongheaded, for it must make any president reluctant to reveal anything, for fear he will be held to have "waived" his privilege altogether.

As to whether and at what stage the privilege (if it exists at all) becomes invalid in an impeachment proceeding, I stand in some doubt, and can do no more for the reader than open the issues.

To begin, it seems that the privilege has a stronger claim in the earlier stages of the impeachment process than in the later. An investigation in its earlier stages may often be rather diffuse, and the close relevance of any given material may be correspondingly less obvious. By the time of the Senate trial, it should be much more sharply clear what bearing any particular matter has on the issues as now precisely drawn.

Further, one must distinguish between two quite different reasons underlying claims of presidential confidentiality. First, it may be claimed that *particular substantive information* cannot be divulged without harm to some vital national interest—predominantly national security. Secondly, it may be claimed that, regardless of the sensitive character of the substantive information, disclosure of conversations will impede the processes of consultation in the White House, since participants must always feel on parade, if they know that revelation of what they say can easily be compelled by any committee of Congress or by a court, and their perhaps tentative positions then publicized.

The second of these reasons may not be good enough to defeat the claim of the Senate (to take the strongest case) to the information it needs in an impeachment trial. It seems inevitable that the first reason—substantive national security—still has room for operation, even at that level. Suppose, for example, that a president were to be charged, in Articles of Impeachment, with having dangerously denuded the United States of its defenses, on some occasion of international tension. That charge could not be plumbed without delving into the most secret aspects of the military establishment— including, it might be, data on the deployment and capacity of our nuclear submarines. I should think that, in such a case, it might well be the plain duty of the president to decline to furnish this information at a trial, where its dissemination could not adequately be controlled.

In sum, my own views on presidential privilege are not now the received ones, and as a practical matter it seems unlikely that the Houses of Congress will concede the privilege much scope in an impeachment proceeding. But a temporary wide agreement on such issues does not authoritatively settle them; a presidential claim of privilege might therefore still be made in good faith. If it were made, some of the questions just explored would become relevant.

The Final Responsibility of Congress

We are used to confiding (or to imagining we confide) all constitutional questions to the courts. I shall later maintain that "judicial review" has no part to play in impeachment proceedings. For now, it should be briefly pointed out that, if I am right, then Congress, in acting on the matters just discussed and on those to be discussed in the next chapter, rests under the very heavy responsibility of determining finally some of the weightiest of constitutional questions, as well as a great many important and difficult questions of procedure. For this purpose, and in this context, we have to divest ourselves of the common misconception that constitutionality is discussable or determinable only in the courts, and that anything is constitutional which a court cannot or will not overturn. We ought to understand, as most senators and congressmen understand, that Congress's responsibility to preserve the forms and the precepts of the Constitution is greater, rather than less, when the judicial forum is unavailable, as it sometimes must be.

The Place of Lawyers

Impeachment is a matter of law, foursquare and all the way, and lawyers must run the process, as surely as doctors must run the operating room. The Congress can get plenty of lawyers, and the money to pay them with. The position of the president is more problematic. Some may think that it is wrong for public funds to go to the financing of the defense of an impeached president, or of one threatened with impeachment. Yet, if we turn the question around and look at it from another side, do we want the outcome of this most important of proceedings ever to be affected by the president's lack of adequate legal help?

We must understand, also, that the participating lawyers are *advocates*, whose job is to take a side and present it with skill and vigor. Our entire legal system bets a great deal on the proposition that this "adversary" system is the least imperfect way to develop all the truth; the corollary is that we must look on partisanship not as an evil but as a part of the system's working. No one, including the president, can be treated lawfully if he is not adequately represented by counsel committed to him. Intemperate public attacks on lawyers, for the positions they take as advocates, are really attacks on our adversary system of justice. Such attacks are particularly surprising when mounted by other lawyers while legal proceedings are pending.

CHAPTER 3

The Impeachable Offense

We come now to the heart of the matter. What offenses are impeachable? The constitutional categories are "Treason, Bribery, and other high Crimes and Misdemeanors."

"Treason"

Here we are on smooth ground. The Constitution narrowly defines "treason," in Article III:

> Treason against the United States shall consist only in levying War against them, or in adhering to their Enemies, giving them Aid and Comfort.

There is, in short, no reason to think the word means anything other than this in the impeachment passage. This makes irrelevant a great deal of learning (interesting enough in itself) about treasons under English law, except insofar (and that is not very far) as the contemplation of these throws light on the interpretation of the exceedingly narrow American definition. Since the situation in our times has in no way implicated "treason," the subject may be put to one side.

"Bribery"

The first point to be made here is that bribery may mean the *taking* as well as the *giving* of a bribe. At the Constitutional Convention, Gouverneur Morris gave the instance of Charles II, who "was bribed by Louis XIV."

As to both the taking and giving of bribes, several cases that have lately been in the spotlight remind us that the *states of mind* of giver and of recipient are all-important. There is nothing wrong with receiving a campaign contribution from dairy interests; there is nothing wrong in raising the price-support on milk. The question is as to the connection between the two events. An old English judge said that "The Devil himself knoweth not the heart of a man." But courts have to try, and continually do try, to work out the truth about intents and motives, for these are often (in bribery cases as elsewhere) of the very essence of the charge.

Is it "bribery" (or attempted "bribery") to suggest to a federal judge, engaged in trying a case crucial to the executive branch, that the directorship of the Federal Bureau of Investigation might be available? It is not wrong to offer a good district judge an important job. Almost all district judges, almost always, have government cases pending before them, in some number. Again, it is *motive* or *intent* that is crucial and that is hard to prove.

Careful, patient inquiry into and weighing of the facts is essential before one even begins to judge, in cases such as these. Beyond doubt, such cases are suspicious, but suspicion is not enough. On the other hand, it is not always a hopeless task, though it is usually a very difficult one, to establish improper motives on circumstantial evidence. In cases such as those here used as examples, there is nothing a conscientious congressman or senator can do but to suspend judgment until all the evidence is heard and analyzed.

"Other high Crimes and Misdemeanors"

This is the third, catchall phrase in the formula designating impeachable offenses. The reader will hardly need to be told that it must generate, and has generated, great difficulties of interpretation. Some definite things can be said about its extent, but we will be left with an area of considerable vagueness. Let us take the definite things first.

It would be well to start with the one and only discussion of the phrase at the 1787 Constitutional Convention. The day was September 8, 1787, just nine days before the Constitution was signed and transmitted for the adherence of the states. The impeachment provision, as reported out by the last of the convention committees (except the final one charged only with polishing the style of the Constitution), listed "treason and bribery" as the only grounds for impeachment and removal. The colloquy we need to look at was brief, taking perhaps five minutes:

> The clause referring to the Senate, the trial of impeachments agst. the President, for Treason & bribery, was taken up.
> Col. Mason. Why is the provision restrained to Treason & bribery only? Treason as defined in the Constitution will not reach many great and dangerous offences. Hastings is not guilty of Treason. Attempts to subvert the Constitution may not be Treason as above defined— As bills of attainder which have saved the British Constitution are forbidden, it is the more necessary to extend: the power of impeachments. He movd. to add after "bribery" "or maladministration". Mr. Gerry seconded him—
> Mr Madison So vague a term will be equivalent to a tenure during pleasure of the Senate.
> Mr Govr Morris, it will not be put in force & can do no harm— An election of every four years will prevent maladministration.
> Col. Mason withdrew "maladministration" & substitutes "other high crimes & misdemeanors" <agst. the State">

On the question thus altered
N. H— ay. Mas. ay— Ct. ay. (N. J. no) Pa no. Del. no. Md
ay. Va. ay. N. C. ay. S. C. ay.ˈ Geo. ay. [Ayes—8; noes—3.]

This is by far the most important piece of evidence on the original intention with regard to the "other high Crimes and Misdemeanors" phrase. It is true that the proceedings of the Convention were secret (a fact, like the fact that the Supreme Court deliberates in deep secrecy, not often mentioned by those who would have us think that secrecy in public affairs is always wrong). But the men present were representative of their time, and their understanding, at the moment when the crucial language was under closest examination, tells us a great deal about its meaning.

It is interesting first that this passage quite definitely establishes that "maladministration" was distinctly *rejected* as a ground for impeachment. The conscious and deliberate character of this rejection is accentuated by the fact that a good many state constitutions of the time did have "maladministration" as an impeachment ground. This does not mean that a given act may not be an instance *both* of "maladministration" *and* of "high crime" or "misdemeanor." It does mean that not *all* acts of "maladministration" are covered by the phrase actually accepted. This follows inevitably from Madison's ready acceptance of the phraseology now in the text; if "maladministration" was too "vague" for him, and "high Crimes and Misdemeanors" included all "maladministration," then he would surely have objected to the phrase actually accepted, as being even "vaguer" than the one rejected.

On the other hand, Mason's ready substitution of "high Crimes and Misdemeanors" indicates that *he* thought (and no voice was raised in doubt) that this new phrase would satisfactorily cover "many great and dangerous offences" not reached by the words "treason" and "bribery"; its coverage was understood to be broad.

The whole colloquy just quoted seems to support the view that "high Crimes and Misdemeanors" ought to be conceived as offenses having about them some flavor of criminality. Mere "maladministration" was not to be enough for impeachment. This line may be a hard one to follow, but it is the line that the Framers quite clearly intended to draw, and we will have to try to follow it as best we can.

Several other things are to be noted about this colloquy of September 8, 1787. Madison's *reason* for objecting to "maladministration" as a ground was that the inclusion of this phrase would result in the president's holding his office "during pleasure of the Senate." In other words, if mere inefficient administration, or administration that did not accord with Congress's view of good policy, were enough for impeachment and removal, without any flavor of criminality or distinct wrongdoing, impeachment and removal would take on the character of a British parliamentary vote of "no confidence." The September 8 colloquy makes it very plain that this was not wanted, and certainly the phrase "high Crimes and Misdemeanors," whatever its vagueness at the edges, seems absolutely to forbid the removal of a president on the grounds that Congress does not on the whole think his administration of public affairs is good. This distinction may not be easy to draw in every case, but there are vast areas in which it is very clear. And it is perhaps the most important distinction of all, because it tells us—and Congress—that whatever may be the grounds for impeachment and removal, dislike of a president's policy is definitely not one of them, and ought to play *no* part in the decision on impeachment. There is every reason to think that most congressmen and senators are aware of this.

Before we leave this verbal exchange of a September 1787 day, one more little-noticed point must be mentioned. Mason says that we need more grounds for impeachment than treason and bribery alone *because we do not have the "bill of attainder,"* which he thinks to have been a safeguard of the British Constitution. Let us explore this.

The parliamentary bill of attainder, probably more often than not directed at a public official, made past conduct of the person attainted criminal, and imposed punishment for it, without judicial trial and without any necessary reference to prior law or to his offense's being a crime under that prior law. The Framers of our Constitution looked on this procedure with such abhorrence that they prohibited its use not only by Congress but even by the states. In the same clauses of the Constitution, they also prohibited, both as to Congress and as to the states, the passage of any *"ex post facto* law"— a law making past conduct criminal, with the result that a person could be punished for doing something which was not criminal when he did it. It will be seen that these two monstrosities overlap in their coverage, because the "bill of attainder," as said just above, may impose penalties for any conduct, whether or not the prior law dealt with that conduct at all.

Now Mason's assumption—which was not challenged and which seems clearly right—was that the "bill of attainder" prohibition applied to any congressional actions dealing with the president. If this assumption is right, then it must also be true that the prohibition of *"ex post facto"* laws—laws making punishable conduct that was not punishable when committed—is equally applicable to Congress's dealings with the president. If this is right—and I would think it right whether Mason had said what he did or not—then we have established another boundary on "high Crimes and Misdemeanors": that phrase must not be so interpreted as to make its operation in a given impeachment case equivalent to the operation of a bill of attainder, or of an *ex post facto* law, or of both.

When a congressman says, in effect, that Congress is entirely free to treat as impeachable any conduct it desires so to treat, he (or she) is giving a good textbook definition of a bill of attainder and an *ex post facto* law, rolled into one. Our Framers abhorred both these things, and we have never wavered from that abhorrence. It cannot be right for Congress to act toward the president as though these prohibitions did not exist. There may be no way to keep Congress from violating their letter or spirit, but the conscientious congressman has to feel them, in spirit at least, as bounding and confining the operation of the vague words, "high Crimes and Misdemeanors."

I say "in spirit," because the letter of these clauses cannot always apply. As pointed out above, in connection with the question of criminal character of the impeachment proceeding, the words "high Crimes and Misdemeanors" are themselves too vague to satisfy constitutional standards of reasonably clear warning, in criminal statutes as applied in the ordinary courts; in this technical sense, the application of the quoted phrase to concrete cases must often be *"ex post facto"* in practical effect. But the spirit and equity of the bill of attainder and *ex post facto* clauses can to a large extent be followed if we treat as impeachable those offenses, and only those, that a reasonable man might anticipate would be thought abusive and wrong, without reference to partisan politics or differences of opinion on policy. The approximation of this result necessitates exploration of some further issues.

The Relation between Impeachable Offenses and Ordinary Crimes

"Treason" and "bribery" are crimes, whether committed by the president or by anyone else. Is the meaning of the phrase "high Crimes and Misdemeanors" limited to ordinary crimes? Can a president lawfully be impeached and removed *only* for conduct which would also be punishable crime for anybody?

Some have contended for this interpretation. It would be easeful to be able to adopt it, because the vague phrase "high Crimes and Misdemeanors" would thus be lent all the precision of the statute book; agonized attempts properly to limit it, while at the same time leaving it properly ample scope, would be avoided. But I cannot think it remotely possible that this interpretation is right.

Suppose a president were to move to Saudi Arabia, so he could have four wives, and were to propose to conduct the office of the presidency by mail and wireless from there. This would not be a crime, provided his passport were in order. Is it possible that such gross and wanton neglect of duty could not be grounds for impeachment and removal?

Suppose a president were to announce that he would under no circumstances appoint any Roman Catholic to office and were rigorously to stick to this plan. I am not sure that this conduct would be punishable as crime, though it would clearly violate the constitutional provision that "no religious test" may ever be required for holding federal office. I cannot believe that it would make any difference whether this conduct was criminal for general purposes; it would clearly be a gross and anticonstitutional abuse of power, going to the life of our national unity, and it would be absurd to think that a president might not properly be removed for it.

Suppose a president were to announce and follow a policy of granting full pardons, in advance of indictment or trial, to all federal agents or police who killed anybody in line of duty, in the District of Columbia, whatever the circumstances and however unnecessary the killing. This would not be a crime, and probably could not be made a crime under the Constitution. But could anybody doubt that such conduct would be impeachable?

These extreme examples test the overall validity of the proposition that impeachable offenses must be ordinary indictable crimes as well, and I think the proposition fails the test. But the rather extravagant character of the illustrations makes another point: most *actual* presidential misdeeds, of a seriousness sufficient to warrant impeachment, are likely to be ordinary crimes as well. It is somewhat strange, indeed, that the question here being examined has assumed such prominence in our days, because most of the wrongful acts that have been seriously charged against an incumbent president are regular crimes—bribery, obstruction of justice, income-tax fraud, and so on—so that, as to these offenses, the issue under discussion here need not arise.

One important exception may be warlike activity. It seems quite possible that military action, unauthorized by Congress and concealed from Congress, might at some point constitute such a murderous and insensate abuse of the commander-in-chief power as to amount to a "high Crime" or "Misdemeanor" for impeachment purposes, though not criminal in the ordinary sense. But (as I shall maintain later) precedents of the distant and recent past make it hard to establish knowing wrongfulness in most such cases. And the question, specifically, whether the long-secret 1973 Cambodian bombing could amount to an impeachable offense is complicated by the fact that, on its being revealed, Congress, by postponing until August 15, 1973, the deadline for its ending, would seem to have come close to ratifying it. One is sailing very close to the wind when one says, "You may do it till August 15, but it is an impeachable offense."

To resume the main line of thought here, I would conclude that the limitation of impeachable offenses to those offenses made generally criminal by statute is unwarranted—even absurd. But it remains true that the House of Representatives and the Senate must feel more comfortable when dealing with conduct clearly criminal in the ordinary sense, for as one gets further from that area it becomes progressively more difficult to be certain, as to any particular offense, that it is impeachable.

To turn the coin around, it would be comforting to our desire for certainty to be able to conclude, at least, that all regular crimes are impeachable offenses. But a moment's reflection would show that this, too, would produce absurdities. Suppose a president transported a woman across a state line or even (so the Mann Act reads) from one point to another within the District of Columbia, for what is quaintly called an "immoral purpose." Or suppose a president did not immediately report to the nearest policeman that he had discovered that one of his aides was a practicing homosexual—thereby committing "misprision of a felony." Or suppose the president actively assisted a young White House intern in concealing the latter's possession of three ounces of marijuana—thus himself becoming guilty of "obstruction of justice." Or suppose, to take a real instance, that the presidential ladies' wearing of the Saudi Arabian jewels technically constituted a criminal "conversion" and that the president could be shown to have been an "accomplice." Would it not be preposterous to think that any of this is what the Framers meant when they referred to "Treason, Bribery, and other high Crimes and Misdemeanors," or that any sensible constitutional plan would make a president removable on such grounds?

An Affirmative Approach to the Meaning of "high Crimes and Misdemeanors"

At this point, I think, we have to have recourse to an old and quite sensible rule of legal construction. This rule has, expectably, a Latin name, *"eiusdem generis."* This phrase means "of the same kind," and what the rule *eiusdem generis* says is that, when a general word occurs after a number of specific words, the meaning of the general word ought often to be limited to the *kind* or *class* of things within which the specific words fall. Thus if I said, "Bring me some ice cream, or some candy, or something else good," I would think you had understood me well if you brought me a piece of good angel food cake, I would boggle a little, perhaps, if you brought me a good baked potato, and I would think you crazy or stupid or willful if you brought me a good book of sermons or a good bicycle tire pump.

Like all "rules" of interpretation, this one is not applicable everywhere. But it seems quite naturally to apply to the phrase "Treason, Bribery, or other high Crimes and Misdemeanors," and could help us toward identifying *both* those ordinary crimes which ought also to be looked upon as impeachable offenses, and those serious misdeeds, *not* ordinary crimes, which ought to be looked on as impeachable offenses, though not criminal in the ordinary sense.

The catch in applying this *eiusdem generis* rule is the difficulty (sometimes) of correctly pinning down the "kind" to which the specific items belong. In the present case, however, the "kind" to which "treason" and "bribery" belong is rather readily identifiable. They are offenses (1) which are extremely serious, (2) which in some way corrupt or subvert the political and governmental process, and (3) which are plainly wrong in themselves to a person of honor, or to a good citizen, regardless of words on the statute books.

Now this all may sound unbearably abstract, but this line of thought could solve many problems. Take the string of imagined cases used above to show the absurdity of limiting impeachable offenses to ordinary crimes—the examples of a president's migrating to Saudi Arabia, or of his excluding Roman Catholics from appointment to office, or of his systematically pardoning all government police who kill anybody under any circumstances. Is it not the fact that these are serious assaults on the integrity of the processes of government, obviously wrong to any man of normal good sense, that makes us feel certain they must be impeachable offenses? On the other hand, take the common crimes that I gave as examples of criminal offenses which we would probably not think impeachable—transporting a woman for "immoral purposes," or easing things a bit for aides in trouble. If you agree with me that these offenses ought not to be held impeachable, is that not because they are not (as treason and bribery are) serious offenses against the nation or its governmental and political processes, obviously wrong, in themselves, to any person of honor?

Let us test the power of this kind of thought by applying it to a far from fanciful set of facts. Suppose a president were shown by convincing evidence to have used the federal tax system consistently and massively as a means of harassing and punishing his political opponents. As far as I know, this conduct is not criminal in the ordinary sense. But does such gross misuse of what is supposed to be a politically neutral arm of government not tend seriously to undermine and corrupt the political order? Is it not obviously wrong, to any man of ordinary honor? If these questions are answered "yes," then this offense, as lawyers might say, is *eiusdem generis,* of the same kind, with treason and bribery. It if *is* a crime under statute, then it is the kind of ordinary crime that ought to be held impeachable. If it is *not* a crime under statute, then it is the kind of offense which ought to be held impeachable, though not criminal in the ordinary sense. In both cases, this is because such an offense is, in the relevant ways, of the same kind as treason and bribery.

This rule will not work all the way; rules of interpretation rarely do. But the one obvious exception may be more apparent than real. Many common crimes—willful murder, for example—though not subversive of government or political order, might be so serious as to make a president simply unviable as a national leader; I cannot think that a president who had committed murder could not be removed by impeachment. But the underlying reason remains much the same; such crimes would so stain a president as to make his continuance in office dangerous to public order. Indeed, it may be this *prospective* tainting of the presidency that caused even treason and bribery to be made impeachable. So far as *punishment* goes, we could punish a traitorous or corrupt president after his term expired; we *remove* him principally because we fear he will do it again, or because a traitor or the taker of a bribe is not thinkable as a national leader.

Now this has been a long pull, but we have our hands on a good first approximation to a rational definition of an impeachable "high Crime or Misdemeanor." Omitting qualifications, and recognizing that the definition is only an approximation, I think we can say that "high Crimes and Misdemeanors," in the constitutional sense, ought to be held to be those offenses which are rather obviously wrong, whether or not "criminal," and which so seriously threaten the order of political society as to make pestilent and dangerous the continuance in power of their perpetrator. The fact that such an act is also criminal helps, even if it is not essential, because a general societal view of wrongness, and sometimes of seriousness, is, in such a case, publicly and authoritatively recorded.

The phrase "high Crimes and Misdemeanors" carries another connotation—that of *distinctness of offense.* It seems that a charge of high crime or high misdemeanor ought to be a charge of a definite act or acts, each of which in itself satisfies the above requirements. General lowness and shabbiness ought not to be enough. The people take some chances when they elect a man to the presidency, and I think this is one of them.

While on the topic of the relations between criminality and impeachability, let me remind the reader that the president, like everybody else, is generally bound by the criminal law. If something he has done is both a crime and an impeachable offense, then, by express constitutional provision, he may, after removal, be tried again in the ordinary courts, and punished; this provision was put in to avoid any possible plea of "double jeopardy." If his criminal act is not held impeachable, it is still criminal. If the contention is upheld (and

I for one think it ought to be) that an *incumbent* president cannot be put on trial in the ordinary courts for ordinary crime, and if the crime he is charged with is not an impeachable offense, the simple and obvious solution would be either to indict him and delay *trial* until after his term has expired, or to delay *indictment* until after his term, with the "Statute of Limitations," which bars prosecution after a certain time, "tolled"—that is to say, stopped running—until the president's term is over. All these results could easily be attained by legitimate judicial techniques, but a simple Act of Congress could put the matter beyond doubt.

Application to Particular Problems

In what follows, I do not intend in any way to judge any real-life issue. Questions of exact fact and of evidence are always crucial, and it is not in any case my wish here to decide anything. But some questions are inevitably suggested by events, and can be dealt with tentatively.

BRIBERY

There is of course no problem about the impeachability of bribery; as indicated above, the problems in such cases are factual and are at their most difficult when motivation is concerned—the motivational connection between the thing of value received and the benefit conferred.

INCOME-TAX FRAUD

Serious income-tax fraud by a president, particularly when the vehicle of such fraud is a set of papers resulting from his holding one government office, and when he might anticipate virtual immunity from serious audit because of his occupying the presidency, would seem definitely impeachable, in addition to being criminal. The offense seems akin to bribery, in that it uses office for corrupt gain; in any case, it undermines government, and confidence in government. A large-scale tax cheat is not a viable chief magistrate.

USE OF TAX SYSTEM TO HARASS OPPONENTS

This has been discussed just above, as an illustration of the partial irrelevance of the ordinary criminal law to the finding of an impeachable offense. This offense not only thoroughly satisfies the canon of interpretation I have tried to elaborate, but also strikes close to the heart of what the Framers most feared in a president—*abuse of power.* Enforcement of any law, including the tax laws, must be to some extent discretionary. Perhaps the most dangerous (and certainly the most immoral) line of conduct an official can follow is that of using this discretion, which is given him for public purposes and is meant to be used neutrally, for the grossly improper purposes of menace and revenge. I should think that clearly evidenced and persistent misconduct of this kind is impeachable beyond a doubt.

Obviously, the same would be true of the harassing use of any governmental power meant to be neutrally employed; the tax system is only a conspicuous example.

IMPOUNDMENT OF APPROPRIATED FUNDS FOR THE PURPOSE OF DESTROYING AUTHORIZED PROGRAMS

I, myself, feel no doubt that it is a violation of his constitutional duty for a president to use his discretionary power (which sometimes must be given him) over expenditures, for the improper purpose of dismantling altogether, or severely crippling, programs that have been regularly enacted in lawful form; this seems to me a violation of his duty to take care that the laws be *faithfully* executed. "Faithfully" is a word that does not keep company with the disingenuous pretense that economy is the motive, when the real motive is hostility to the law.

But that is only an opinion, and this is a gray area, wherein opinions may legitimately differ. The president operates under a statutory directive that total expenditure or debt not exceed a certain figure, and he may even have some residual responsibility not to see the country descend into financial ruin. He might think (though others would disagree) that these responsibilities were to be served best by cuts where his judgment advised they might least hurtfully be made, rather than by cuts across the board. Many appropriations, moreover, are phrased by Congress as *authorities* rather than as *duties* to spend. Finally, there seem to exist, in many cases, adequate judicial remedies for persons or governmental units who have a clear legal right to the "impounded" money, and a president might think that by "impounding" he is doing no more than referring a doubtful question to the courts.

On the whole, for all these reasons, I incline to think "impoundment" not an impeachable offense, though one ought never try to anticipate judgment on the flagrancy of some instance that might come to light. The problem is one that badly needs to be dealt with by Congress, using means short of impeachment—as to which, see Chapter 5.

UNAUTHORIZED WARLIKE OPERATIONS

This I find the most agonizing question of all. As a new matter, I should have thought that totally unauthorized entrance into hostilities, without any emergency or any immediate threat to the nation, was the grossest possible usurpation of power, clearly impeachable.

Unfortunately, it is not a new matter. The Bay of Pigs, for example, happened—and as far as I recall there was no talk of impeachment. There are many, many other precedents to which appeal can be made. Furthermore, there is often some fairly plausible claim of authorization in the particular case, and where experts disagree on justification, it is hard to find clear and wanton abuse of power. Moreover, it is the undoubted fact that the wrongness of unauthorized military action is likely to seem clear, on the whole, only to those who disapprove substantively of the particular intervention; would it be thought that an impeachable offense had been committed if our forces in the Mediterranean were ordered to intervene to keep the Syrians from taking Haifa?

Reluctantly, I have to conclude that only a very extreme and not now visible case ought to bring the impeachment weapon into play as a sanction against presidential warlike activity. Congress ought to deal with this matter comprehensively and clearly; if it did, then the president's violation of the congressional rules would be impeachable beyond a doubt, for the uncertainties generated by precedent would be cleared up. The so-called War Powers Resolution passed last year is so far from filling this need that the Administration, not without plausibility, could publicly toy with the idea that the resolution, supposedly a restraint on the president, actually authorized resumption of the Cambodian bombing that Congress had earlier ordered to be ended!

IMPROPER CAMPAIGN TACTICS

I know of no offense the impeachability of which more depends on the exact case shown by evidence. There must come a point at which the deliberate harassment of political opponents—the bugging of their offices, the circulation of known lies about them, the attributing to them of statements they never made, and so forth—takes on the character of deliberate and knowing wrong, as highly corruptive of the political process as is the actual bribery of voters. On the other hand, politics is known by all not to be croquet, and a certain amount of roughing up is expected. One could construct an endless series of hypothetical cases, and try to pronounce on each; the part of wisdom, in any such situation, is to suspend judgment until a real case is made out.

Here again, Congress could do much more than it has done to make clear what the rules are to be.

OBSTRUCTION OF JUSTICE

Here the question has to be whether the obstruction of justice has to do with public affairs and the political system; I would not think impeachable a president's act in helping a child or a friend of his to conceal misdeeds, unless the action were so gross as to make the president unviable as a leader. In many cases his failure to protect some people at some times might result in his being held in contempt by the public. I would have to say that the protection of their own people is in all leaders, up to a point, a forgivable sin, and perhaps even an expectable one; this consideration may go to the issue of "substantiality," with which this chapter closes. But the obstruction of justice is ordinarily a wrong as well as a crime, and when it occurs in connection with governmental matters, and when its perpetrator is the person principally charged with taking care that the laws be faithfully executed, there must come a point at which excuses fail. Here again, the concreteness of the evidentiary case is all-important.

Some Final Considerations

THE PRESIDENT'S RESPONSIBILITY FOR
ACTS OF HIS SUBORDINATES

As to each possible impeachable offense, the question may arise of the president's responsibility for his people's misdeeds.

Here I think we have to remember that it is the *president* who must be found guilty of "high Crimes and Misdemeanors." A simple attribution to him of everything done by persons working under him is totally incompatible with the flavor of criminality, of moral wrong, in the quoted phrase. No chief of any considerable enterprise could pass such a test.

At the other extreme, it goes without saying that the president (like anybody else) is totally responsible for what he commands, suggests, or ratifies.

The difficult area is in between, the area of "negligence." I would find it impossible to qualify simple carelessness in supervision as a "high Crime or Misdemeanor"; perfect freedom from negligence is for the angels. At this point, however, the general law furnishes us with a valuable concept. When carelessness is so gross and habitual as to be evidence of *indifference* to wrongdoing, it may be in effect equivalent to ratification of wrongdoing. If I drive my car in an utterly reckless manner, and someone is injured, the case is not merely that I have been guilty of "negligence," but that I have so behaved as to show indifference to whether somebody got hurt or not. Gross and habitual indifference of this kind is more than mere negligence, and might well be held to amount to impeachable conduct.

Here, as in so many cases, everything depends on what the evidence in a case actually shows, but these are the right lines along which to sort out the evidence.

GOOD-FAITH BELIEF IN THE RIGHTNESS OF AN ACT

This concept has figured in this book at several points, in the discussion of particular offenses. Belief in the lawfulness or rightness of an action, in order to be a defense, must be such belief as a reasonable person could hold. A reasonable man could think selective impoundment of funds both lawful and right, but no reasonable man could think it right to use the tax system for partisan political purposes.

Here, again, Congress has an enormous role to play. A clean-cut declaration, by Congress, that a given line of conduct is wrong, makes it much more difficult for a reasonable man to claim reliance on his own assessment of the matter. Congress has the power, within wide limits, to make presidential conduct criminal; where this was done, no subsequent president could be heard to say that he was not fully warned.

SUBSTANTIALITY

"Not all presidential misconduct is sufficient to constitute grounds for impeachment. There is a further requirement—substantiality." These words occur in the Conclusion to the House Judiciary Committee's Staff Report on Constitutional Grounds for Presidential Impeachment (the full citation is in the Bibliography).

Undoubtedly this is true, but the concept is an extremely difficult one to handle. Does it mean "substantiality of the single offense" or "substantiality of all offenses proved, taken together"? Either alternative is dangerous. Should a president be impeached and removed when he has committed no single offense which would in itself justify removal? Would not an affirmative answer encourage the "stacking" of rather petty charges? On the other hand, would a president who has committed a number of offenses, offenses that,

one by one, satisfy every criterion for impeachability except substantiality, not at some point have shown himself unfit for office?

To me, the first of these dangers is by far the greater, for it merges
with fatal ease into the peril of an overall judgment of mere unfit-
ness—quite outside the plain meaning of "high Crimes and Misdemeanors." The question will present itself in any particular case in
highly concrete form. The answer, when answer must be given, must
probably be to some extent political; law can lead us to the point
where "substantiality" becomes the issue, but law cannot tell us what
is "substantial" for the purpose of decision. We may justifiably hope
that those who have to make this political judgment will see it as
high-political, and not as having any connection with partisan politics, or with views on policy.

A Note on History

The phrase "high Crimes and Misdemeanors" comes to us out of
English law and practice, starting (as far as we know) in 1386. It
frequently figured in impeachment of officers. The English history
seems to establish with some clarity that the English did not understand the phrase as denoting *only* common crimes, but in some
sense saw it as including serious misconduct in office, whether or
not punishable as crime in the ordinary courts. Beyond that, I have
to confess that I can read no clear message. Sometimes the English
cases seem to prove too much, treating as "high Crimes and Misdemeanors" petty acts of maladministration which no sensible person
could think impeachable offenses in a president, or in anybody. This
leaves us right where we were, so far as line-drawing is concerned.
In many cases, "impeachment," a charge brought by the House of
Commons, was not followed by conviction in the House of Lords,
the finally responsible body; this makes the precedent a truncated
one at best. Further, although many of the Framers of our Constitu-

tion undoubtedly knew in at least a general way of the English usage, and certainly borrowed the term "high Crimes and Misdemeanors" from that usage, it is hard for me to think that many of them, or many people at the state ratifying conventions, or many members of the late eighteenth-century American public, could have carried about, ever-present in their minds, much of the superabundant learning which in modern times has been developed on the subject. Nor does that learning, interesting as it is intrinsically, seem to me to eventuate in the unequivocal validation of any very precise view of the exact boundaries of the phrase's meaning.

If this history were to be canvassed here, this would be a very different (and much fatter) book—and I would be a very different (and probably much leaner) person. I have to say, on my own responsibility, that the English historical material I have seen does not seem to stand in the way of our working out, in any great case in our own times, a sensible concept of the meaning of "high Crimes and Misdemeanors," suitable to the spirit and structure of our Constitution.

All the American precedents are handily collected in the above-mentioned report by the staff of the Committee on the Judiciary of the House of Representatives, 93rd Congress, 2nd Session, *Constitutional Grounds for Presidential Impeachment*. But these precedents, too, fall far short of furnishing a well-rounded and well-supported answer to the question of the meaning of "high Crimes and Misdemeanors." There have been thirteen impeachments in all. Ten of them were of federal judges; four of these were acquitted, four were convicted, and two resigned, with the result that no Senate verdict was given. One senator was impeached; the Senate voted that it had no jurisdiction to convict a senator on impeachment, so that the case was dismissed without verdict. One secretary of war was impeached; he was acquitted on all Articles, but the force of the acquittal is clouded by the fact that an indeterminate number of senators may (or may not) have voted to acquit dominantly or wholly on the ground that the man had already resigned. The remaining case was that of President Andrew Johnson. He was impeached, substantially, for having removed the secretary of war, a holdover from Lincoln's administration, in alleged violation of a Tenure of Office Act passed by the Reconstruction Congress, and for attempting to bring disgrace and ridicule on Congress—itself a ridiculous charge. He was acquitted, but by a vote just one short of the two-thirds needful to convict; such an "acquittal" is not a satisfactory legal precedent on "impeachable offense."

Now it is very plain that these American precedents speak with little clarity to new issues. Like the English precedents, they pretty clearly show a pattern of going beyond ordinary crimes for impeachable offenses: intoxication on the bench, for example, figures in several of the judicial impeachments. On the other hand, an acquittal blunts any precedent.

In the one presidential case, that of Johnson, the acquittal was almost certainly not on the facts, but on the belief that no impeachable offense had been charged—but with the weakness as precedent just mentioned. Moreover, the Johnson impeachment is, to say the least, by no means universally regarded today as a paradigm of propriety or of unimpassioned law.

On the whole, again, what this history really says is that no historical impediment exists to a sensible, reasoned treatment, right now, of the problem of the meaning of "high Crimes and Misdemeanors." The history of impeachment, like the history of most serious subjects, may conduce to underlying wisdom, but decision is for us, today.

CHAPTER 4

Impeachment and the Courts

Is There to Be Judicial Review of the Senate's Verdict on Impeachment?

The process of presidential impeachment, and trial thereon, culminates in a judgment of the Senate, either that the president is not guilty, or that he is guilty on one or more of the Articles of Impeachment voted by the House, and is to be removed from office (perhaps with the additional penalty of disqualification to hold office in the future). Is this judgment of conviction final, or is it in some manner appealable, to the Supreme Court or elsewhere?

Now before we take this question apart technically, let us just sit back a moment and consider the straight sense of it. The most powerful maxim of constitutional law is that its rules ought to make sense. Let us try to imagine the situation which could be produced by providing judicial review of a senatorial judgment of removal.

Picture, if you will, a president whose conduct has attracted such unfavorable notice as to be thoroughly investigated by the Judiciary Committee of the House of Representatives. The result of this investigation has been a formal recommendation to the whole House that Articles of Impeachment be voted. After the fullest debate, with the attention of the country focused on the issue, the House concludes that the president ought indeed to be impeached of "Treason, Bribery, or other high Crimes and Misdemeanors." All questions of law and fact have now been thoroughly canvassed in one House, with a result adverse to the president. Next, the Articles of Impeachment go to the Senate, which is put upon special solemn oath, and which sits in judgment with the chief justice of the Supreme Court presiding. The Senate, after plenary trial and fullest argument of counsel, and after debate among senators on fact and law, votes by a two-thirds majority to convict and remove the president.

The president now appeals to the Supreme Court. The jurisdiction of that Court over the appeal is to say the least quite unclear, but it takes jurisdiction anyway. On the merits, the Court disagrees with the House and with the Senate on some point, let us say, as to the meaning of "high Crimes and Misdemeanors," or on some procedural question of weight (perhaps dividing 5 to 4, perhaps filing nine opinions no five of which espouse the same reasoning). *So it puts the impeached and convicted president back in for the rest of his term.* And we all live happily ever after.

I don't think I possess the resources of rhetoric adequate to characterizing the absurdity of that position. With what aura of legitimacy would a thus-reinstated chief magistrate be surrounded? Who would salute? When a respectably dressed Londoner approached the Duke of Wellington, saying "Mr. Smith, I believe," the Duke replied, "If you believe that, you'll believe anything." I would say the same of anyone who can believe that there is hidden away somewhere, in the interstitial silences of a Constitution formed by men of practical wisdom, a command that could bring about such a preposterous result as the judicial reinstatement of a president solemnly convicted, pursuant to the constitutional forms, of "Treason, Bribery, or other high Crimes and Misdemeanors." (I may say, parenthetically, that if you are one who believes that sound constitutional law cannot make nonsense, or generate absurdities, you can rest on that correct belief and skip the rest of this chapter.)

If such a result seemed to be commanded by explicit language in the Constitution, then I should think the Supreme Court would try desperately to find some loophole through which to escape exercising this absurd function. But the Constitution contains no such command. The command has to be worked out, if at all, on the basis of elaborate inference piled on inference.

The standard justifications of judicial review do not support it. Courts decide constitutional questions when these arise in cases over which they have jurisdiction. The Supreme Court, as a quick perusal of Article III will show, does not have "original" jurisdiction over any kind of suit seeking to overturn a senatorial judgment removing the president. The question of its "appellate" jurisdiction (the jurisdiction to hear and decide appeals) is more complicated. On the face of Article III, the Supreme Court has "appellate" jurisdiction over all the cases brought within the judicial power by that Article. One of these categories is "all Cases, in Law and Equity, arising under this Constitution. . . ." If the Supreme Court's appellate power over impeachment judgments is located anywhere, it is here.

Many objections to its being found here come readily to mind. The terms "Law" and "Equity" were and are thoroughly established terms of art, referring to the two sorts of regular judicial courts existing, in England and here, at the time of the adoption of the Constitution; impeachments are, in this well-known technical sense, neither in "Law" nor in "Equity." This reading chimes exactly with the whole tenor of Article III, which has to do with regular judicial business in ordinary courts, except for a passage making it clear that jury trial was to play no part in impeachment. This latter provision, as a study of successive drafts of the Constitution will show, was left in the judiciary Article (now Article III) when impeachment trial was shifted from the Supreme Court to the Senate, and therefore to the

Article (now Article I) dealing with the legislative branch. (The chief importance of this shift is discussed below.) It was doubtless left in place because its main thrust—a general rule of trial by jury—belonged in the judiciary article, and the reservation on impeachments had to be left in it, lest there be misunderstanding. The occurrence of the word "impeachment" in the judiciary Article (III) has therefore no tendency to establish that impeachment is in any way an Article III matter. Indeed, close algebraic reasoning would lead to the conclusion that impeachment, and trial thereon, are not within the Article III "judicial power" at all, for that "judicial power" is a power that Congress may "vest," in the first instance, in inferior courts of its own creation (except as to cases, of which impeachment is not one, which are within the Supreme Court's "original" jurisdiction), and it cannot do that as to impeachment proceedings.

There is no inconsistency here with the position I have taken, above, that the trial in the Senate is to be looked on as *similar* to a "judicial" trial, and that senators should perceive their role in these terms. A trial that is "judicial" in the sense that it aims at fairness, impartiality, and decision according to law, need not, for that reason, fall within the Article III "judicial power," which concerns, up, down, and sideways, the jurisdiction of ordinary courts of justice.

Further support here is found in the fact that, when the Constitutional Convention moved the trial of impeachments from the Supreme Court to the Senate (as to which removal see below) it dropped "impeachment" altogether from the list which later became, by stylistic revision, the list defining the Article III "judicial power."

But these algebraic reasonings, which are really alien to the spirit of constitutional law, need not be mathematically conclusive; they need show no more than that there is an escape, thank Heaven, from the preposterous situation that we would face if the Constitution unmistakeably commanded judicial review of convictions on impeachment.

There are other, lower roads of escape. As it came from the hands of its draftsmen, the present Article III of the Constitution might appear affirmatively to grant appellate jurisdiction (jurisdiction to hear appeals) to the Supreme Court:

> In all the other Cases before mentioned [i.e., those within the federal "judicial power"], the supreme Court *shall have* appellate Jurisdiction, both as to Law and Fact, *with such Exceptions,* and under such Regulations as the Congress shall make. (Emphasis added)

But the entire history of the Supreme Court's appellate jurisdiction, as shaped by Congress's exercise of its own "exceptions" power, unequivocally disaffirms this interpretation. It has been held with invariant uniformity, since the beginning, that the comprehensive and detailed Acts of Congress *granting* appellate jurisdiction to the Supreme Court, in carefully named classes of cases (Acts which are now part of a painstakingly considered codification), by implication *except* from that jurisdiction all cases *not* named, and that these jurisdictional Acts thus exercise, as to all cases not named by them, the congressional power to make *"exceptions"* to the Supreme Court's appellate jurisdiction—a power expressly given to Congress in the part of Article III just quoted. Thus, in practical effect, the Supreme Court does *not* exercise appellate jurisdiction unless Congress grants that jurisdiction in a statute; every single appeal ever filed in the Supreme Court begins with a paper wherein it is indispensable that the *congressional statute* giving jurisdiction be cited. Of course Congress has never included, in any such statute, a grant to the Supreme Court of appellate power over senatorial judgments in impeachment cases. It is quite reasonable, then (even if one believes, as I never could, that impeachment verdicts fell within the Article III appellate judicial power before Congress acted), to hold that Congress has "excepted" it, so that it cannot be exercised.

Even if both these arguments fail to convince, at least the "exceptions" power remains, and Congress might at any time exercise it to *remove* impeachment matters from the appellate jurisdiction of the Supreme Court. The one Supreme Court precedent on this subject held that Congress could effectively abolish the Court's jurisdiction over an appeal *even after it was filed and argued.* The very fact that Congress could do this strengthens the position that the judicial appellate power never extended to impeachment verdicts, for it would be a virtual nullity, hardly worth the labor of constructing, when Congress could knock it down at will.

All these arguments are strongly buttressed by the fact that the 1787 Constitutional Convention, after debate and over prestigeful opposition, moved impeachment trials out of the Supreme Court and into the Senate. This was done, as one would expect, for the quite straightforward reason that the Convention thought the Senate, rather than the Supreme Court, should deal with impeachments. Why else?

So far as I can find, not one syllable pronounced or written in or around the time of the adoption of the Constitution gives the faintest color to the supposition that the Supreme Court was expected to have anything to do with impeachments, or the trial thereof, or appeals thereon.

What about the lower courts? Suppose a convicted and removed president were to bring a civil action in the Federal District Court for the District of Columbia seeking a judicial declaration that he had been wrongfully convicted, and asking for a mandatory injunction (perhaps against Congress and the White House Guards as parties defendant) commanding his reinstallation in office.

Now the lower courts are *created* by Congress, under Article III, and their jurisdiction is wholly controlled by Congress. The District

Courts (and I apologize for being so solemn about this matter, but if I can I want to lay it to rest once and for all) have jurisdiction (*conferred upon them by Congress* in pursuance of Article III) over civil actions, wherein the amount in controversy is over $10,000, "arising under the Constitution and laws of the United States." Is the convicted (and assumedly ex-) president's suit one of that description? Cases "arising under" maritime law, although that law is now firmly considered a part of *national* law, made so by the Constitution, have been held not to be suits "arising under" the Constitution or laws of the United States, on the quite sensible ground that, regardless of the breadth of the statutory language considered abstractly, the history of the subject makes it most unlikely that Congress ever intended to include maritime cases within this general language. Is it possible to say any less than that of the claim of a removed president to be reinstated, or even to get his salary? Is it so much as conceivable that Congress, in putting this general language ("all civil actions arising under the Constitution . . .") on the statute book, intended to give the lower federal courts jurisdiction to annul and undo impeachment verdicts? (Here, again, Congress might easily at any time take away the jurisdictional grant, if there were any realism in the fear that a court would try to trap Congress in this way.)

There is, so far as I can find, not a shred of affirmative historical evidence that the Framers and ratifiers of the Constitution ever thought for one moment that the *lower* courts were to deal with impeachment questions. It is quite incredible, given the great amount of attention paid to impeachment procedure, that this possibility never would have been mentioned, if in fact it had been thought a serious possibility.

Now as a practical matter no court is ever going to succeed in putting an impeached and convicted president back in office; it is most unlikely that any court will try. The only thing that could result from a judicial attempt to do this would be a terrible constitutional crisis. For the ultimate latent weakness of judicial power (kept latent only by the courts' respect for the law that creates them) is that the duty to obey a judicial decree exists only when the court that utters the decree is acting within its jurisdiction. This rule is sensibly softened by some concession to courts of the right to determine their own jurisdiction. But a court acting in wide excess of its jurisdiction has no claim to being obeyed. If the Supreme Court, or any other federal court, were to order reinstatement of an impeached and convicted president, there would be, to say the least, a very grave and quite legitimate doubt whether that decree had any title to being obeyed, or whether it was, on the other hand, a decree as widely outside judicial jurisdiction as would be a judicial order to Congress to increase the penalty for counterfeiting. To cite the most frightening consequence, our military commanders would have to decide for themselves which president they were bound to obey, the reinstated one or his successor. I think I would advise them that they must obey the successor; others would undoubtedly give the contrary advice. Is it possible that our Constitution set up such a situation as that?

I have thought it worthwhile to argue this point fully because, while I cannot conceive that any court would so have lost the faculty of judgment as to try to undo a Senate sentence of removal on impeachment, I think it well that, so far as possible, the fundamental unconstitutionality of such action be publicly accepted, precisely because, as I have briefly pointed out above, the wide diffusion of this concept—that the courts have no role to fill—makes very plain to all the *final* responsibility of the Senate, on facts and on law. It would be most unfortunate if the notion got about that the Senate's verdict were somehow tentative. The crucial senatorial vote should be taken, and should be known to be taken, with full knowledge that there is no appeal. No senator should be encouraged to think he can shift to any court responsibility for an unpalatable or unpopular decision.

The dissemination of the "judicial review" idea could be most unfortunate in another way; if a removed president tried it, and had his case (as would almost surely happen) dismissed for want of jurisdiction, he might be able, though quite wrongly, to persuade a part of the people that he had been denied his rightful day in court.

I would conclude, then, with a paraphrase of the well-known saying of the country banker, when he was asked about cashing a check for a stranger. He said, "There are ten rules about cashing checks for strangers. The first rule is, 'Never cash a check for a stranger.' The other nine rules don't matter." There are ten rules about judicial review of the judgments of the Senate on impeachments. The first rule is that the courts have, in this, no part at all to play. The other nine rules don't matter.

May Congress Use the Federal Courts to Assist in Impeachment Investigations?

This question stands on a very different footing. It might very well happen, for example, that the House of Representatives Judiciary Committee, or some other committee charged with investigation that might lead to impeachment, would need the aid of judicial process to procure testimony or documents. For example, a recalcitrant witness might be jailed by court order, on application of the committee, until he agreed to testify. The practical and jurisdictional complexities here are many, but these complexities need not be explored here. The point is that no general *constitutional* objection prevents Congress from enlisting the aid of the courts in ways ancillary to its own responsibilities.

Some problems, however, are salient and pervasive. Once any matter (such as, to pursue the example just given, the use of the judicial civil contempt power to compel testimony) is brought into court, the one thing Congress cannot do is to tell the court how it must decide the case. A court, for example, might conclude that the witness was privileged *not* to testify, and free him. To this extent, Congress (very properly) loses control of its own business when it brings that business into court.

Secondly, judicial proceedings are *timed* largely as the judges see fit; in consequence, bringing business into court means surrendering one's own timing plan.

These considerations probably will prevent any very frequent recourse by either House of Congress to the courts, for aid in impeachment proceedings. Each House has a considerable inherent power to punish for contempt, without recourse to the courts.

CHAPTER 5

Short of Impeachment

In some tribal cultures, the system of legal sanctions is very simple. There are two possible ways of dealing with deviants: toleration and death. A persistent troublemaker is endured for a long time, perhaps not without grumbling, but without any effective attempt at control. Then he commits some action which is just one thing too many—the last straw. After some informal consultation, he is speared, or shoved out into the cold to freeze. There is only one sanction—the sanction of elimination. No finer-graded system of control is conceived.

Sometimes we seem to be talking as though a system something like that were all we have for dealing with a president or with the presidency. A great many people are dissatisfied with what the presidency has become and is becoming. We feel things have gone too far. So we start consulting among ourselves, and at last reach for the spear of impeachment.

Of course it can be true that things may have gone too far in any given case. Elimination may in a rare case be the only way. But we have, let us hope, a long future to face together, we and our presidents. It might be well to consider whether a more finely graded system of controls might be developed.

Events have shown that the presidency, however much its incumbent may aspire to and scheme for strength, is actually quite weak, without means of defense against a resolute Congress. The spectacle has perhaps not edified. But it has demonstrated, to a pathological degree, something which is a good thing in smaller amounts: the presidency has little firm constitutional power of its own. A skimming of the Constitution confirms this all the way. The president's power to appoint officers is in the hands of the Senate. The commander-in-chief power is subject to such control as inheres in Congress's powers to declare war, to raise and support the armed forces, and to enact regulations for their governance. The "foreign relations" power is deeply bitten into by Congress's power over foreign commerce, while power over the internal economy could be made plenary through exercise of Congress's power over commerce among the states, and of its power to tax and spend "for the general welfare." And underlying everything is the congressional power to appropriate (or to refuse to appropriate) the money that makes the political world go 'round.

In brief, Congress is by no means in the position of having to sit idly by, counting up grievances, until time comes to call a council of elders and sharpen the impeachment spear. Congress (as is perfectly plain on the face of the Constitution) can exercise just about any control it wants on the operations of government, including, in vast measure if not entirely, the actions of the president.

Correspondingly, Congress must share the responsibility for the twentieth-century aggrandizement of the presidency. Much of congressional complaint about that aggrandizement is shadowboxing, or at best a wail for the vanished horse, emanating from a man who habitually and chronically just would not lock the stable door.

Take the matter of war. The Viet Nam war went on a long time. There was continual complaint in Congress. Why didn't Congress refuse to appropriate money for prosecuting the war? That refusal couldn't even have been vetoed, because it would not have been a congressional action, but a congressional inaction. Why didn't Congress pass a concurrent resolution (which, being a mere statement of congressional opinion, is not subject to veto) declaring in unmistakeable terms the view that the war was immoral and against the country's interest? Would not such a resolution, though without legal force, have destroyed the moral basis of the war, to an extent making virtually necessary its speedy liquidation? Maybe not, but would there have been any harm in trying?

Consider the matter of "impoundment"—the refusal by the president to spend appropriated money on programs not to his liking. Many of the statutes in question are quite unclear as to whether the expenditure is bindingly directed or merely authorized. Congress has not yet passed a general law clarifying the limits on the president's power to "impound," though such a statute, unquestionably constitutional, would greatly clarify the guidelines confining a presidential power which is to some extent necessary.

Why should Congress not pass a law, with severe penalties for all concerned, stringently forbidding the use of the income-tax system to harass political enemies—or its use for any purpose other than revenue-raising, with the rain of audit falling at random on friends and "enemies" alike?

There has been much concern about the use of public funds for what are essentially personal purposes, such as the upkeep and repair of the president's houses. This matter is plainly amenable to legislative control; no president would dare veto an Act setting bounds on this, and if he did, and if passage over his veto failed, it would still be possible for Congress to refuse further appropriations for these purposes.

One could go on like this all day. Congress is top dog—if (and what an enormous if) it wants to be.

Let us take the more complex matter of *information*. A great deal of Congress's weakness comes from its not having developed a system for procuring a continual flow to itself of information of all kinds from the departments and agencies. This has little to do with presidential "confidentiality"; I am not talking now about the president's own conversations in the Oval Office, but about data on wheat production in the Department of Agriculture. Almost none of such information is even arguably "privileged" against congressional access and use. The task is for Congress to create the conduits and reservoirs to bring in and hold ready this information. Knowledge is power, above all in politics; Congress cannot be innovative and creative unless it insists on having fluid access to the knowledge now stored in the agencies and departments.

Or take the possible use of the concurrent resolution, not subject to veto, as a means of expressing formally both the convictions and the intentions of Congress. I have already mentioned how such a resolution, though without force as law, might have destroyed the moral basis for the Viet Nam war. Might it not in other cases be used to censure, or to register some more mildly worded disapproval of, actions of the president? Is it conceivable that such censure, by a Congress to which the president must look for support, would have no effect?

In the long haul, we must put the spear of impeachment back in the closet, though coated with cosmoline against rust. There are infinitely numerous milder ways in which the elephantiasis of the presidency can be treated.

We need, too, to rehabilitate the presidency. It is an office that on the whole has served us well. It is in bad shape.

But that is another story. The most critical point possible in the relations of Congress and the presidency is that of the actual imminence of impeachment proceedings. If this book has a single thought underlying all its particularities, it is that, when this most critical of points is reached, it is utterly vital to the health of our polity that the needful proceedings, whatever their event, be handled lawfully. Perhaps the most important thing the citizen can strive for, in this context, is an appreciation of the constraints which this need for visible and faultless lawfulness puts upon those bodies—the House and the Senate—who are charged with responsibility. On the foundation of that lawfulness, and on it only, a better future may be built.

PART II

Philip Bobbitt

CHAPTER 6

Recent Precedents

Charles Black's essay was written during the constitutional crisis provoked by the efforts of Richard Nixon's presidential campaign to corrupt the processes of the 1972 election. Since then, we have experienced several other tremors of varying force in the landscape of impeachment.

Doctrinal arguments in constitutional law are developed case by case, following rules laid down in precedents. Very few actions by the Congress are governed by doctrine, but the Congress's—and the president's *constitutional* decisions—are subject to a similar sort of doctrinal analysis as those of courts or other legal institutions. As in common-law doctrine, the rule of "last in time" prevails (recent precedents are more salient than older ones), but the significance to be accorded these precedents varies with the authority of the decider. The 1999 impeachment and acquittal of President Bill Clinton carries more authority than the abortive attempt by a state legislature in 2008 to bring about impeachment proceedings against President George W. Bush, even though the latter is more recent. And what is the significance, if any, of the attempted impeachments against Presidents Ronald Reagan and Barack Obama? Can we infer that the legal bases for these indictments—respectively, the creation of a secret, privately funded covert action capability and the refusal to enforce congressional mandates regarding narcotics and immigration—were constitutionally inadequate? Or that the facts simply didn't support the claims of high crimes, assuming these charges amount to such infractions?

There is something to be learned from the doctrinal history of presidential impeachments since 1974, but perhaps the most important development has been the transfer of influence from the organs of governmental decision-making to the public. Black's essay emphasized the solemnity of the American trial process and cautioned that "a snow of telegrams ought to play no part" in it. The taking of polls regarding guilt or innocence would be "an unspeakable indecency." That position, however faithful to the history, text, and structure of the impeachment provisions, is harder to maintain today.

What has changed is ourselves: we no longer have the confidence in the leadership of Congress that we had in the Nixon era, and impeachment is a supremely congressional action (indeed one reason we have lost that confidence is the fiasco of the Clinton impeachment by the House). Moreover, owing to the zeal of some (and perhaps the self-absorption of others), we have compromised the habits of decorum, fastidious withholding of judgment, impartial procedures, detachment from partisanship, and insistence on fundamental fairness that Black thought necessary to the due process of impeachment. We are more inclined to treat impeachment as a political struggle for public opinion, waged in the media, and less like the grand inquest envisioned by the Constitution's Framers. The "vigilant waiting" urged by Black is less acceptable to a citizenry inflamed by its political divisions and uncertain as to the competence of its institutions.

There remains, however, this hope: that our people come to believe, even more than they believe the superiority of their own opinions, that the best means of realizing their preferences, and of preserving the values on which they believe their preferences to be based, lies in the working of legal institutions whose legitimacy depends on shared understandings, not sheer partisan political power. If this becomes the ethos of the new century, then the precedents still to be formed will restore Black's reverence for the due process of impeachment as it stood in 1974, poised before the abyss.

Nixon and Watergate

On February 6, 1974, one year after a Senate committee convened its investigation of a burglary at the Democratic campaign's Watergate headquarters, the House of Representatives passed a resolution authorizing the House Judiciary Committee to determine if grounds existed to bring a Bill of Impeachment against Richard Nixon. Following a subpoena from the special prosecutor as part of a grand jury inquiry, on April 30, 1974, the White House released to the House committee edited transcripts of tapes made of Oval Office conversations. When the special prosecutor pressed for unedited transcripts and additional conversations, the White House refused on grounds that the recordings were protected from compelled disclosure by executive privilege. On July 24, however, the Supreme Court ordered the president to comply with the subpoena. The pace quickened. On July 27, 29, and 30, the committee approved three proposed Articles of Impeachment and sent them to the full House. Before the House could vote, Nixon on August 5 released an incriminating tape that triggered a collapse in his support in Congress. He resigned on the 8th.

Does Nixon's resignation create a precedent, even though there was no impeachment and conviction? What is the scope of that precedent? Is it coextensive with the charges in the Bill of Impeachment?

At a minimum, we can dismiss two proposed counts that were not referred to the full House: one charging the president with misleading the Congress regarding the secret bombing of Cambodia, and one alleging a failure to pay appropriate income taxes. There is little doubt that making war in the absence of an imminent hostile attack must occur with the acquiescence of Congress, but there was some doubt whether the administration, by informing senior congressional officials, had constructively informed the larger membership as well. It was also not clear whether a particular bombing campaign within a larger, authorized war might be within the prerogatives of the commander in chief, at least in the absence of congressional action to the contrary. The president's failure to pay taxes is not in itself a high crime or misdemeanor because it is unrelated to his official duties; this count also decisively failed in the committee.

The three Articles of Impeachment sent to the House charged that the president obstructed the investigation of the Watergate burglary (adopted by a committee vote of 27–11); that he engaged in a pattern of conduct that violated various rights of individual citizens (adopted 28–10); and that he refused to cooperate with the committee by providing materials when requested (adopted 21–17). Of these three proposed Articles, the most we can say is that the president apparently judged at least one of them a sufficient basis for his resignation, thus giving Nixon's resignation the vague status of a plea bargain negotiated in advance of an indictment—or perhaps what is called an *Alford* plea, wherein a defendant while asserting his innocence admits that the evidence is sufficient for him to be found guilty. In this case, a president effectively preempted indictment—impeachment—by voluntarily accepting the penalties that would have accompanied his conviction.

Thus the effective constitutional consequences of the Nixon precedent presume that at least one of the three counts was legally and factually sufficient for the president's removal from office. Moreover, and more decisively, we know from multiple sources that by

August 5, 1974, following the release of incriminating conversations recorded in the Oval Office, more than two-thirds of the Senate votes needed for conviction were committed against the president.

We can eliminate the third count as a precedent because the offense of contempt of Congress, on which Article 3 of the Bill of Impeachment was based, would have been cured by the release of the tapes and transcripts requested by the House Judiciary Committee, which, in the event, led to the president's resignation. That leaves Articles 1 and 2, both of which charged Nixon with having violated his oath of office and the requirement of Article II of the Constitution that he faithfully execute the laws. The basis for this charge in Article 1 lay in the president's impeding, delaying, and obstructing the investigation into the attempted theft of materials from the Democratic campaign headquarters (which he was not charged with planning). Article 2 charged a violation of much the same duties in four separate spheres: violating the rights of citizens through IRS audits and the unauthorized sharing of personal data, and through surveillance outside that authorized by lawful authority; interfering with Department of Justice (DOJ) and CIA operations to effect a cover-up of White House officials' involvement in the break-in; failing to report what he knew once he learned about the break-in; and creating a special intelligence unit in the White House. There is ample historical evidence, based primarily on statements by Nixon's Republican defenders in the House, that Article 1 would have commanded broad support. The support for Articles 2 and 3 was less definitive.

Dealing with congressional doctrine much as we might parse the judicial opinions of a multimember panel, we can say that Nixon's resignation stands for the proposition that where agents of a presidential campaign have violated the law in order to acquire political intelligence, and where the president, whether or not he was aware of the scheme, subsequently engages in a course of conduct intended to impede or mislead investigation of this illicit operation—such as by counseling witnesses to issue false statements, promising or paying "hush money" to potential witnesses, making false statements to US officials, withholding evidence, promising favorable treatment for silence, or making false statements to the public—there is a sufficient predicate for impeachment.

Thus, far from eviscerating the precedent, or at least creating no new doctrine, as would have been the case had the charges been withdrawn before the House could vote on them, the president's own conduct stands for the recognition that the gravamen of at least one of the charges satisfied Article II's requirement of a "high crime" against the Constitution.

Reagan and Iran-Contra

For the increasingly fraught relationship between Congress and the president today, the Watergate affair is the gift that keeps on giving. One such gift is the legacy of the Church Committee, convened in 1975 to explore the Nixon administration's illicit use of the intelligence agencies, which had been uncovered by the Senate Judiciary Committee in its Watergate investigation. The Church Committee examined CIA and FBI abuses more broadly, including the improper monitoring of American citizens' political activities as well as various sensational intrigues abroad. In the aftermath of the ensuing revelations, Congress enacted various statutory and regulatory restraints on covert action—and pressed for a restrictive executive order promulgated by the Ford administration—that many intelligence professionals felt hampered their ability to compete effectively against foreign adversaries.

By the 1980s, US covert operations faced a funding cutoff in Central America and risked exposure there and elsewhere from congressional committees that were, by law, required to be informed of these secret plans. This conflict with the Congress occurred against the backdrop of a rise in anti-American terrorism in the Near East and the apparent inability of US clandestine operations to penetrate and neutralize the groups responsible. Throughout 1984 and 1985, the United States was the target of bombings, assassinations of its diplomats, hijackings of sea- and aircraft, and, ominously, a wave of kidnappings originating in the stateless chaos of Lebanon. The traditional methods of counterterrorism, which depend upon firm local authority and careful police work, seemed impossible in such circumstances. The Reagan administration struggled to secure the release of hostages, several of whom were tortured and killed. Despite its failure to protect its agents, the administration steadfastly refused to pay ransoms. Thus the country was genuinely shocked to learn from a report first published in a Lebanese magazine that a secret mission, headed by the president's former national security advisor, had traveled to Iran to do just that. The mission was sent to negotiate a ransom payment by means of the sale of otherwise-embargoed US missiles to the Iranian regime.

When Justice Department officials, who thought they were investigating a relatively simple arms-for-hostages scandal, stumbled upon a memorandum that quite casually listed the Nicaraguan Contras, a right-wing insurgency against that country's elected socialist government, as recipients of profits from the illicit arms transactions, the effect on the public was electrifying. It appeared not only that the president had been lying about ransoming hostages—"America will never make concessions to terrorists," Reagan had asserted in a news conference in June 1985—but that he had taken the opportunity presented by the ransom deal to divert funds to aid the Nicaraguan insurgency in defiance of US statutes forbidding such assistance. When the Senate select committee appointed to investigate the affair began its work in early 1987, the public and the Congress believed they already had a relatively clear picture of the facts in the Iran-Contra scandal. This picture was depicted in the report of the Tower Commission, whose account went as follows: the president, in a desperate effort to rescue American hostages held captive in Lebanon, had agreed to sell hitherto embargoed arms to the Iranian government; because these weapons were procured at wholesale cost to the US government and sold at a black market price to the Iranians, they brought a substantial profit; instead of being returned to the US Treasury, these profits were then "diverted" to the Contras. The question of the hour was: Did the president know about this diversion?

This focus on the diversion reflected a mistaken assumption among the president's political enemies that only a violation of the US Criminal Code could serve as grounds for impeachment. They seized on the diversion as the most promising basis for such a charge. If the president had contrived to misappropriate funds that properly belonged to the Treasury by authorizing that the profits from the sale of US war materiel be sent to the Contras, then proof of this would serve as the predicate for his removal from office. The House majority staff conducted an investigation that appeared to be based on these assumptions. Interestingly, and with perhaps greater insight, the president's closest counselors were also willing to stake their hopes on the outcome of a contest over the president's knowledge of the diversion. They believed that the president would not have paid much attention to what was little more than an accounting method.

In fact, the constitutional violation was far more profound than the diversion. The more serious offense lay in the development of a quasi-private covert action capability of which the diversion was merely a minor side effect. A privatized, off-the-books covert action agency offered the administration several important advantages. First, the outsourced agency could manage the Contra insurgency, fulfilling the oversight role played by the CIA before its funding and participation were curtailed through a series of statutes. The privatized agency would avoid the unwelcome scrutiny of Congress because it would not be subject to congressional funding, and this too was thought to enhance the secrecy of its projects. Second, such an agency could act more daringly, avoiding the legal restraints of executive orders that it would be embarrassing to repeal. It could defy certain international norms against reprisal because it would not be definitively associated with the US government. Thus it might recapture the initiative that the United States seemed to have surrendered to terrorist groups. Finally, the agency's apparent detachment from the official government would afford the president plausible denial of US responsibility should the agency's operations be exposed. Statutes adopted in the late 1970s required that the president verify in writing the necessity of each covert operation and inform congressional oversight committees about them. These laws had greatly increased the political risk of these operations, since the president's authorization might always be exposed after he had issued a public denial.

There was, however, a fundamental constitutional problem with this bright idea. Article I provides the link between government operations and the democratic mandate by requiring that all funding take place by statute, that is, by the actions of elected officials who can be turned out by the voters every biennium. In attempting to circumvent Article I by relying on nonappropriated funds, no matter how noble his purpose and no matter how beneficent the source, the president was striking at the Article's role as the very foundation of our democratic system. Article I provides the check on the actions of the federal government provided by the biennial election of members of the House.

This error in attempting to use nonappropriated funds is compounded by the solicitation of operating funds from foreign governments with whom the federal government alone has institutional economic, security, and diplomatic relations. In some cases, where the "donating" country is the recipient of federal assistance, the solicitations amount to little more than kickbacks, and the executive avoids congressional oversight because the money comes from the assistance program budget. Moreover, the United States can become subject to blackmail when the donating regime threatens to expose the scheme.

The *Federalist Papers* do not treat this exotic subject directly, but a relevant discussion can be found there. In *Federalist* #26, Alexander Hamilton observed: "It has been said that the provision, which limits the appropriation of money for the support of an army to the period of two years, would be unavailing: because the executive, when once possessed of a force large enough to awe the people into submission, would find resources in that very force sufficient to enable him to dispense with supplies from the acts of the legislature." In the same essay, Hamilton had discounted this concern, asserting the profound importance of biennial elections for maintaining control through appropriations. This seems to underscore the centrality of the appropriations process, even and perhaps especially in the arena of national security.

In the event, nothing happened. The president went on television and vaguely apologized for not appreciating that his scheme to release American hostages could be perceived as a ransom. The "Enterprise," as one of the conspirators had named the private covert-action entity, was not discussed. Without some appreciation of what was at stake, the idea of impeachment faded with the inability to prove the president had himself directed the diversion. A tree had fallen in the forest, but even those that heard it did not recognize it as such. Article 2 of the Articles of Impeachment against Richard Nixon adopted by the House Judiciary Committee had charged that the president had "authorized and permitted to be maintained a secret investigative unit [which was privately] financed which unlawfully utilized the resources of the Central Intelligence Agency, [and] engaged in covert . . . activities." But no connection was drawn between this charge and the privately financed, covert action agency set up by the National Security Council under President Reagan.

Moreover, nothing compelled the Congress to go further. A decade later, some members of Congress would argue that the Constitution gave the House no discretion not to impeach the president if he had committed high crimes and misdemeanors, but this erroneous insight lay in the future.

While there is no doctrinal precedent to be inferred from this travesty, it would be idle to suppose that the secret privatizing of federal functions ended with the Iran-Contra affair. It waits, hidden in the groundcover of constitutional misapprehension, and will no doubt stir again as market mechanisms replace agency regulations as a preferred means of governmental operations.

Clinton and Gingrich

What is the scope of the precedent created by the Clinton impeachment if, as in the Andrew Johnson impeachment, the Senate refused to convict? Does the refusal to convict cast doubt on the legal sufficiency of the indictment, given that the principal facts were not really at issue?

On November 5, 1997, well after the independent counsel Robert Fiske had determined that Bill Clinton and his wife had not acted improperly in the collapse of an Arkansas bank and land development scheme known as Whitewater, and well before the confidante of a former White House intern secretly taped the intern's revelations of a brief affair with the president, a Georgia congressman introduced House Resolution 304 along with seventeen cosponsors. This resolution called for an investigation to determine whether there existed grounds for Clinton's impeachment, though none of its claims ever made it into the Bill of Impeachment (of which the congressman became a House manager), or into the report of the independent counsel who succeeded Fiske, which provided the basis on which Clinton was impeached. Nevertheless, the resolution caught the affronted mood and the venom evoked in many by the president and the exhilaration of the effort, nurtured by the Speaker of the House, to contrive the president's removal. The history of the Clinton impeachment is not one of an unfolding, escalating disclosure of the president's maneuvers, like Watergate, but rather a largely fortuitous combination of parallel legal moves actuated not so much by events as by an obsessive ambition to remove Clinton from the White House by whatever means could be found.

Parallel lines of inquiry linked the independent counsel's Whitewater investigations and a private civil suit, financed by the president's political opponents, over an alleged sexual advance. Both scandals, if that's what they were, occurred when Clinton was governor of Arkansas, before he became president. Had either strand played out on legal grounds, there might never have been an impeachment proceeding. The independent counsel never found any evidence of wrongdoing with respect to the Whitewater matter, and sexual misconduct is not, in itself, an impeachable offense, barring some nexus between this behavior and the president's official duties. It was only when these two lines of attack were studiedly brought into intersection that a trap could be laid for the president, tempting him into false testimony that might conceivably serve, it was thought, as a predicate for impeachment.

The Whitewater scandal erupted into the national consciousness when a *New York Times* story—which did not charge the Clintons with anything unlawful—was suddenly supercharged by the suicide, in late July 1993, of a deputy White House counsel and former law partner of the first lady in Little Rock. Republicans in the Congress pressed for the appointment of an independent counsel to investigate Whitewater and its relationship to this death. Perhaps convinced that he had not behaved improperly, the president asked the attorney general to appoint such a counsel. Because the statute authorizing the office of the independent counsel had expired, she made the appointment on the basis of her authority as head of the Justice Department, choosing a prominent Republican lawyer, Robert Fiske. After a six-month investigation, his office issued a final report dispatching claims of foul play in the death of the deputy counsel. As for the Whitewater charges, Fiske's report amply sustained an independent study commissioned by the regulatory body overseeing the reconstitution of failed banks, which had cleared the president and former governor.

After Congress reauthorized the independent counsel statute, a three-judge panel appointed Kenneth Starr, a respected former solicitor general, to go over the same ground. Starr spent three years investigating Whitewater and was unable to find any prosecutable wrongdoing by either the president or Mrs. Clinton. When he submitted his final report to the House Judiciary Committee to urge impeachment, he scarcely mentioned the Whitewater matter. Instead, he offered the results of a lengthy investigation into charges of sexual misconduct by the president.

A former White House employee, who befriended a former White House intern and became her confidante, began secretly taping their conversations at the suggestion of a literary agent who was prominent among anti-Clinton partisans. Part of the conversations concerned sex the intern had had with the president. Frustrated at her inability to insinuate reports of the president's misconduct into mainstream news outlets, the confidante gave the story to lawyers representing a former Arkansas state employee, Paula Jones. Jones had brought suit against the president alleging crass sexual behavior while he was governor, and the suit eventually morphed from an effort to restore the plaintiff's self-respect into an effort to harass and humiliate the president. This lawsuit eventually brought together various anti-Clinton forces who, though they wished to drive the president from office, probably never thought this would be accomplished through impeachment based on Jones's claims, which were ultimately dismissed by the trial court.

This picture changed in early January 1998, when a former law school classmate of one of the members of the group financing the Jones suit, went to work for the independent counsel. Informed about the secret taping, the independent counsel authorized contact with the confidante and also sought approval from the DOJ and the panel that had appointed him to expand his jurisdiction on the grounds that a friend of the president, allegedly linked to the Whitewater investigation, had also attempted to help the intern find post-government employment. Starr's deputy apparently falsely assured the deputy attorney general that there had been no contact with the Jones attorneys. When the expanded authorization was given, events quickened. Clinton was due to be questioned by Paula Jones's attorneys just two days later, on January 17, and they now could ask him about the intern. The day before this deposition, the intern's confidante led her into an ambush: FBI agents and three of the independent counsel's deputies confronted her at a hotel in Arlington, Virginia. There seems little question that, as a postmortem by the Department of Justice later put it, lawyers for the independent counsel exercised poor judgment in negotiating with the former intern without her counsel present. Preventing her from informing her lawyer about the trap into which she had been lured, however, was essential to ensnaring the president. In a sworn deposition on January 17, 1998, Clinton denied having sexual relations with the intern; claimed he could not remember ever having been alone with her; and permitted his lawyer to state on the basis of an earlier, false deposition by the intern that there was no sex in any manner between the two. Starr concluded that Clinton had committed perjury and submitted his findings to Congress.

That report itself was without precedent and, especially in light of the ultimate resolution by the Senate, should not serve as a model for future reports by either independent counsels (authorized by statute) or special counsels appointed by the Department of Justice. Leon Jaworski, when he was a special prosecutor in the Watergate matter, scrupulously sent to the House only a few factual files on President Nixon, accompanied by no recommendations whatsoever. Starr, instead, urgently pressed the House to impeach Clinton, both in his report and in testimony to the House Judiciary Committee. The Judiciary Committee conducted no real hearings of its own, choosing instead to rely on the independent counsel's report as a basis for impeachment.

The full House considered four charges. The bases of these charges were that the president had (1) abused his office by using staff to facilitate sexual liaisons with other personnel, (2) used his office to buy silence by offering jobs or threatening to embarrass others, and (3) lied under oath and given false statements to the public to cover up his misconduct and thus to obstruct the pursuit of a lawful investigation and prosecution (which supported two of the charges).

The House ultimately adopted two Articles of Impeachment: perjury to a grand jury, and obstruction of justice. Two other Articles failed: the second count of perjury in the Jones case, and one accusing Clinton of abuse of power. A trial in the US Senate began immediately after the seating of the 106th Congress. A vote of 67 senators was required to remove Clinton from office. In the event, 50 senators voted to convict the president on the obstruction of justice charge and 45 voted to uphold the perjury charge. No Democratic senator voted guilty on either charge. Thus Clinton, like Andrew Johnson, was acquitted on all charges.

In their summations, neither counsel for the president nor counsel for the House managers addressed the issue of whether the president had committed a constitutional crime: whether a nexus had been shown between his official duty to uphold the Constitution and a concerted effort by him to imperil the country through acts that undermined his unique duties as president.

It may well be that, two decades later, in the atmosphere of public outrage over sexual misconduct by powerful men, Bill Clinton would have been driven from office by his own party. Does that mean that the constitutional law of impeachment has changed? Does greater sensitivity to rather crass and manipulative sexual behavior elevate that behavior to a crime against the perpetuation of the order and ethos of the State, even accepting that such predations have enormous political and cultural consequences?

It is sometimes said nowadays that no corporate board member would hesitate to remove a CEO found guilty of the president's behavior. The Senate, however, is not a board of directors, and it does not appoint the president. If we know little about how the Framers and ratifiers of Article II would answer this corporatist question, we know this: they decisively rejected removal of the president for simple maladministration, and they rejected also the subordination of the president to the Congress that such a power would imply. But do their intentions really matter when we have a new, perhaps more equitable consciousness? Or should that consciousness be reflected in elections rather than in prosecutions and trials conducted by the Congress? The aggressive change to more confrontational tactics between the branches of government initiated and championed by the Speaker of the House at the time of the Clinton impeachment is still with us, even to a heightened degree. The news media's adversarial mode (I have in mind the *New York Times* as much as any cable news channel) was much in evidence in the Clinton catastrophe and is with us still. But the Democrats who rallied around the president then would be in a very different position today.

It is true that they protected the presidency from a fortuitous conspiracy that would have changed the balance of constitutional power between the branches. Starr even wanted to make the exercise of executive privilege an impeachable offense—as did the equally aggressive members of the Judiciary Committee during Watergate. Perhaps the Democrats were at fault for failing to find common ground with their Republican colleagues by forcing a resignation—as the Republicans did to Nixon—especially since there was a competent vice-president in the wings who had also been elected by the American people.

Ultimately, the Clinton impeachment carries very little doctrinal or precedential authority, because the House indictment was decisively rejected by the Senate and because of the indictment's peculiar grounds. If the answer to the wrong question is not a wrong answer but no answer at all, then the questions put to the Senate by the prosecution established no rules for the future. There is a cautionary tale here, but its lessons are largely negative. They urge us not to repeat this disgraceful episode.

If, for example, the president were knowingly to make bombastic and false statements in public, or in private to his subordinates, that were neither crimes in themselves nor related to his performance in office, he should not be entrapped by federal officials asking him whether he knew the statements to be untrue or be forced to reiterate them in sworn testimony. Only if the false statement is part of a concerted effort to commit an impeachable offense—that is, a constitutional crime—can such deceits serve as the predicate for impeachment.

There are, however, less substantive issues as to which the Clinton impeachment did provide precedents. One was whether a Bill of Impeachment adopted by the House of one Congress is sufficient to trigger a trial in the Senate after a new Congress has convened—or whether a new bill must be voted by the House. In the ordinary course of legislation, if a bill passes only one house before a Congress ends, it must be reenacted by both houses of a new Congress in order to be sent to the president for signing. In the case of Andrew Johnson, the Bill of Impeachment was passed by the House and tried by the Senate during the same Congress. In the Clinton case, a new Congress might have made a difference, as the new House had more Democrats, and the second Article of Impeachment barely passed the old House—although in the event the new House continued to back the impeachment managers. But the Senate chose to rely on Thomas Jefferson's *Manual of Parliamentary Practice*—written when Jefferson presided over the Senate as vice-president—and the precedents of judges impeached and tried by different Congresses. Because the Senate could have decided the other way, we may take the Clinton precedent to be that a House from one Congress can validly refer an impeachment to the Senate of another.

The Senate formulated an initial set of rules governing proceedings in the run-up to President Johnson's impeachment, and that framework largely survived through the Clinton trial. In 1935, the Senate amended these rules to include what is now Rule XI, which provides:

> That in the trial of any impeachment the Presiding Officer of the Senate, if the Senate so orders, shall appoint a committee of Senators to receive evidence and take testimony at such times and places as the committee may determine.

Charles Black disapproved of this measure, arguing that the text of Article I—"the Senate shall have the sole Power to try all impeachments"—left no scope for subgroups. His views were not rejected in *United States* v. *Nixon* so much as left open, when the Supreme Court accepted the argument that the Senate's power to try impeachments included the nonreviewable discretion to determine how to conduct its trials. This is consistent with the court's jurisprudence that it should avoid expressing opinions on matters delegated to other branches. During the Clinton impeachment trial, evidence was presented to the whole Senate, not to a Rule XI committee, and so it is probably correct to say that the constitutionality of such committees—at least where the presidency is at stake—remains untested. The Senate may well be the final determinant of its own rules, but its recent practice suggests some ambivalence about employing Rule XI procedures in a presidential impeachment.

The impeachment and acquittal of Bill Clinton in 1998–99 are the only comprehensive precedents for the impeachment process since the impeachment and acquittal of Andrew Johnson in 1868, which was itself the first impeachment of the president since the creation of the office of the presidency in 1789. Accordingly, the Clinton debacle, from which no one walked away unscathed, will shape the development of the impeachment clauses more than any other events to date, including the Nixon resignation. This development gives reason for concern, for it reflects the effects of concerted attempts to criminalize American politics, weaponizing our legal processes by evading or even discarding the constitutional bases of those processes. Clinton's impeachment may be partly responsible for the contempt in which many Americans hold their political institutions.

Bush and the Iraq War

On February 19, 2008, the New Hampshire House of Representatives took up House Resolution 24, a bill to petition Congress to commence impeachment proceedings against President George W. Bush and his vice-president, on charges that included taking the United States to war against Iraq. The New Hampshire House had heard testimony supporting "a legal theory that a state legislature can in fact force the US House to begin impeachment proceedings." This theory was based on "section 603 of Jefferson's *Manual of Parliamentary Practice* [which] states that an impeachment may be set in motion by the United States House of Representatives by charges transmitted from the legislature of a state."

The New Hampshire proceedings appear to have arisen from several embedded confusions. Jefferson's *Manual* was created from materials he assembled and used as an aid when presiding over the US Senate. They included notes he took while a student at William and Mary College as well as his comments on British parliamentary procedure, and he augmented them throughout his tenure as vice-president. He published them as a single work, intended for future vice-presidents, in 1801; a second edition with added material was printed in 1812. Although prepared for the US Senate, the *Manual* was formally incorporated by the House of Representatives into its rules in 1837.

The sponsors of the New Hampshire resolution calling for the impeachment of President Bush appeared to have relied on House commentary on Jefferson's *Manual,* not as they claimed on his actual text. That text provides that "the Commons, as the grand inquest of the nation, becomes suitors for penal justice. The general course is to pass a resolution containing a criminal charge against the supposed delinquent, and then to direct some member to impeach them by oral accusation, at the bar of the House of Lords, in the name of the Commons." The commentary adds that "in the House various events have been credited with setting an impeachment in motion: . . . A resolution introduced by a Member and referred to a committee . . . ; Charges transmitted from the legislature of a State or territory or from a grand jury; or facts developed and reported by an investigating committee of the House."

There are several problems here: the text relied upon is not Jefferson's *Manual*; even if it were, the *Manual* is an authority for the rules of the House only to the extent that these have not been modified by later precedents; and in any case the *Manual* was written for the Senate and is largely a commentary on British parliamentary practices of the time, which, with respect to the grounds for impeachment, are quite irrelevant. Furthermore, no rule of the House could possibly force the House to commence impeachment proceedings. House rules can always be changed or amended by the members, and more importantly, any compulsion is probably incompatible with the provision of Article I, section 2, clause 5 that the "House of Representatives shall have the sole Power of Impeachment." Perhaps for these reasons, some commentators have mocked the New Hampshire resolution and its sponsors.

This would be a mistake. While it was an error to purport to rely on Jefferson's *Manual*, the commentary on the *Manual* on which the authors of the resolution should have relied is, if anything, more relevant than the original provisions of the *Manual*. That commentary cites Volume 3 of *Hinds' Precedents of the House of Representatives of the United States,* sections 2469 and 2319, which do indeed appear to offer precedents in which referrals from the legislature of a state or territory have served as the basis for Congressional consideration of an impeachment inquiry.

On February 20, 2008, the New Hampshire bill was ruled "Inexpedient to Legislate," and it was tabled on April 16, never to be revived. But in an era in which the federalism of the US constitutional structure has empowered more assertive state legislatures, and as the US population continues to sort itself geographically by political and cultural preferences, this route to impeachment may someday be reactivated.

Obama and Executive Discretion

Two developments—the appearance of cities and states that refuse to cooperate with federal immigration officials, and the legalization of marijuana by many states despite federal narcotics laws criminalizing its use—are harbingers of a deeper change in the constitutional order of the American State, to which I alluded in the preceding section. The increasing polarization and paralysis of Congress only speeds this change. What if the president, unable to push his reform agenda through the Congress, simply refused to enforce the laws he could not get repealed? Would that constitute an impeachable offense?

One of the proposed charges drafted by the House Judiciary Committee at the time of the Nixon impeachment was the claim that the president had refused to spend appropriated funds for projects and operations to which he was opposed on grounds of policy but that had been passed over his opposition and sometimes his veto. This charge of "impoundment" turned on the president's intent. It was not uncommon for presidents to decline to spend funds authorized by the Congress; Thomas Jefferson had done so in 1801, and the power was generally regarded as inherent in the executive. Jefferson's case involved his refusal to spend money authorized for the acquisition of warships for the US Navy. He reported that "the favorable and peaceable turn of affairs on the Mississippi rendered an immediate execution of [the authorized funds] unnecessary." Nixon, however, used impoundment to override congressional policies with which he disagreed. He had tried to impound funds for an environmental project that he had opposed and then vetoed, and to which his veto had been overridden. In the end, the Judiciary Committee refused to forward to the whole House the charge of impoundment as a separate impeachable offense. Later, in *Train* v. *City of New York* (1975), the Supreme Court held that the impoundment power cannot be used as a kind of irrefutable veto.

For my part, I believed at the time that impoundment could provide a strong predicate for impeachment when the president used his discretionary power over expenditures for the purpose of dismantling or crippling programs regularly enacted in lawful form. Charles Black, however, was careful to call this a "gray area." The president might think that if cuts were needed to ensure fiscal stability, they ought to come where they might be least hurtful. Moreover, Black noted, many appropriation statutes authorize but do not mandate spending. Anticipating *Train*, he concluded that the president might believe that by impounding funds he was merely referring a doubtful matter to the courts.

The Obama presidency was criticized for a not dissimilar tactic: using its prosecutorial discretion to decline to enforce statutes with which the president disagreed. In 2009, the Department of Justice simply ceased enforcing federal narcotics laws against persons whose actions complied with "existing state laws providing for the medical use of marijuana." But the most far-reaching of the administration's actions in this vein was the president's decision, announced on June 15, 2012, not to enforce the removal provisions of the Immigration and Nationality Act against an estimated 800,000 to 1.76 million persons who were illegally present in the United States.

The criteria used by the Obama administration tracked those proposed by the Development, Relief, and Education for Alien Minors Act (DREAM Act), first proposed in 2001, which Congress had repeatedly failed to adopt. The constitutional problem for such a presidential strategy arises from Article II, section 3, which provides that the president shall "take Care that the Laws be faithfully executed." In the words of an early nineteenth-century commentator, William Rawle, "Every individual is bound to obey the law, however objectionable it may appear to him: the executive power is bound not only to obey, but to execute." There seems to have been from the very beginning of our constitutional life a consensus that the Take Care Clause imposed a duty on the president to enforce laws whether or not he considered them wise as a matter of policy.

This view of the Take Care Clause is strengthened by the broad language of the Vesting Clause that puts in the hands of the president all "executive Power"—in contrast to the language of Article I, which gives the Congress only those "legislative Powers herein granted," and the even more restricted judicial power of Article III. In light of Article II's broad grant of power, the Take Care Clause can scarcely be an additional grant of authority, and instead is generally read to underscore the responsibility of the president to exercise his power to ensure that the laws of the United States are actually executed.

This construction is further strengthened by the Presidential Oath Clause, which prescribes the following: "I do solemnly swear (or affirm) that I will faithfully execute the Office of President of the United States . . ."

Finally, the history of the adoption of the Take Care Clause at Philadelphia further supports the view that this clause requires the president to enforce the laws adopted by Congress regardless of his view of their merits (excepting constitutionality). As the influential Framer James Wilson, who introduced the draft dealing with Article II, put it some years later, the clause established that the president has "authority, not to make, or alter, or dispense with the laws, but execute an act of the laws, which [are] established."

None of this is to deny that an ineradicable element of the executive function is discretion and the prerogative to carry out the purpose of statutes as effectively as possible. As with impoundment, however, it is a matter of intent. If the president concludes that a lack of available personnel, or contradictory directions from Congress, or changed circumstances compel him to give priority to the enforcement of some provisions and not others, that is one thing. If his argument is not made in good faith, it follows almost ineluctably that the laws have not been "faithfully" executed. As two critics of the administration put it, "for if the president can refuse to enforce a federal law against the class of 800,000 to 1.76 million individuals, what discernible limits are there to prosecutorial discretion? . . . Can a president who wants tax cuts that a recalcitrant Congress will not enact decline to enforce the income tax laws? Can a president effectively suspend the environmental laws by refusing to sue polluters, or workplace and labor laws by refusing to fine violators?"

Before and After

When Alexander Hamilton wrote in *Federalist* #65 that the jurisdiction of impeachment covers "offenses which proceed from the misconduct of public men, or, in other words, from the abuse or violation of some public trust," did he mean that the actions for which an official can be impeached must take place while that person is in office? Presumably a private person—perhaps even one seeking office—is not yet a public person. On this line of thinking, an impeachable offense may be committed only by someone who can be impeached—just as the Code of Military Conduct can be violated only by someone who is or has been in the armed forces. There must be someone to whom the prohibition applies when the act occurs; and by this reasoning, the impeachment of a public official cannot be based on her acts before entering public life.

Supporting this view is the ordinary construction we give to the term "high" in the phrase "high Crimes and Misdemeanors." Like the notorious High Sheriff of Nottingham, or the Lord High Executioner of Gilbert and Sullivan, this term here applies to government officials and their duties. Just as we must distinguish "high Crimes and Misdemeanors" from the ordinary crimes found in statute books, we must be equally careful in determining who precisely is subject to these prohibitions.

It should be noted that in the precedents of the Nixon and Clinton impeachments, the House Judiciary Committee took care to exclude Articles of Impeachment that arose from acts that occurred before their subjects took office.

Those who argue that acts prior to assuming the presidency are relevant to impeachment note that people seeking the office of president must submit to many legal restrictions as to how they run their campaigns, receive money, what their financial disclosures must report, and so forth. If not uncovered during the campaign, violations of such restrictions should be a matter for Congress, it is said, once the conspiracy is exposed. There's something to this, but I don't think that consideration necessarily lies in the role of Congress as the assessor of the legal culpability of the successful candidate—whose criminal conduct, at any rate, can always be prosecuted in the criminal system, even if this must wait until the end of his term.

Some also argue that offenses committed by the civilian, if they are serious enough, would if discovered render the office of the presidency nonviable. Of course that may be true, but this nonviability seems to be political rather than legal, and thus a matter for public judgment, not for trial by a coordinate branch of the government. A congressional judgment of nonviability would bring us perilously close to making maladministration a ground for impeachment—a basis that was decisively rejected at the Constitutional Convention.

And finally it is urged that once in office a president can make investigation of his earlier offenses difficult and time-consuming even if the initial disclosure of these offenses has otherwise undermined his legitimacy. Invoking executive privilege and relying on his authority to control the work of the Department of Justice, a president could rescue an administration that is foundering and ought to be dispensed with. So it is argued that impeachment must be available as a remedy even though the original acts which now occasion such contempt occurred before the inauguration. However strong a motive the exposure of earlier misdeeds might provide for public impatience or even revulsion, it scarcely satisfies a legal standard for prosecution and conviction to say that a great many voters are experiencing buyer's remorse. Our institutions, based on a respect for the rule of law, demand that mercurial judgments of approval are insufficient to overturn the constitutional mandate of a presidential election. Moreover, obstruction that was itself official misconduct could still provide a basis for impeachment even though the incident of the obstruction was not itself an official act, that is, occurred before the president assumed office.

Before offering what I believe to be the best rule to resolve the before/after dilemma, let us look at an actual historical case rather than a series of hypotheticals: the incident of the so-called Chennault Affair that received renewed attention in 2017.

In the autumn of 1968, encouraged by Soviet channels, President Lyndon Johnson decided to offer Hanoi a complete cessation of US bombing in Vietnam, believing that, for the first time, the North Vietnamese were willing to agree to the basic framework the Johnson administration insisted was a precondition for American withdrawal. Having made his decision, he discovered that the Nixon campaign was sending messages to the South Vietnamese ambassador via a prominent Asian-American Republican activist, Anna Chennault. These messages encouraged the Saigon government to refuse to participate in the peace talks then under way by promising that a Nixon administration would take a harder line against Hanoi. Johnson ordered government surveillance of Chennault, the South Vietnamese embassy in Washington, and the president of South Vietnam's offices in Saigon.

The LBJ Presidential Library has made available tapes of conversations between Johnson and Senator Richard Russell that disclose

Johnson's awareness of Nixon's conspiracy. Johnson received FBI surveillance reports detailing contacts between Chennault and the South Vietnamese ambassador in which she advised him she had received a message from Nixon saying, "Hold on. We are going to win. . . . Please tell your boss [the South Vietnamese president] to hold on." LBJ is also recorded telling Everett Dirksen, the Republican leader of the Senate, "I'm reading their hand, Everett. This is treason," to which Dirksen replied, "I know."

Although the election was only days away, Johnson refused to take these revelations to the public. Perhaps he feared that the administration's surveillance of an ally and a candidate for the presidency would poison his successor's presidency, whoever won the election. Without conclusive proof of Nixon's knowledge or collusion that he could make public, Johnson spoke to Nixon directly. "I would never do anything to encourage . . . Saigon not to come to the table," Nixon told Johnson. In a famous interview, he later elaborated: "I did not authorize [Chennault], and I had no knowledge of any contact with the South Vietnamese at that point . . . because I couldn't have done that in conscience." But notes taken by H. R. Haldeman, Nixon's chief of staff, suggest that Nixon was in fact the mastermind behind the conspiracy. These notes record Nixon's direction to Haldeman on October 19 that the South Vietnamese president was feeling "tremendous pressure" from Johnson and that the South Vietnamese wanted the Republicans to determine what the "quid pro quo" would be for their cooperation in stalling the peace talks. Nixon said, "Keep Anna Chennault working on South Vietnam."

What might have happened in the war, or in the election, if this conspiracy had been exposed, one cannot say.

The Chennault Affair contains many strands that my brief account necessarily ignores, but let us assume that the charge against Nixon is accurate: while running for the presidency in 1968, he persuaded a foreign government to delay peace negotiations in order to advance his candidacy. This gives us a paradigm case, because it involves an attempt to pervert the course of an election. Does it matter whether Nixon would have lost the election had his schemes been unsuccessful, or whether he actually swayed the South Vietnamese? Is it enough that he believed the election was in the balance and that his conspiracy might make the difference in a very close race (which it was)? In such a case, the before/after distinction seems beside the point. The constitutionally significant elements in the conspiracy are not confined to Nixon's subsequent acts in public office but clearly include the effects on a public event of great constitutional significance—a presidential election. Perverting the course of an election—or attempting to do so—either by illicit means, such as stealing documents in an effort to embarrass an opponent (as in Watergate), or improper means, such as torpedoing peace negotiations by the existing government, cries out for a clear rule. During the 1787 Philadelphia Convention, Virginia delegate George Mason asked, "Shall the man who has practiced corruption and by that means procured his appointment in the first instance, be suffered to escape punishment, by repeating his guilt?" What rule do we apply if we don't know whether the office was in fact successfully procured by corrupt means? Suppose Nixon would have won anyway? Suppose his collaborators in Saigon didn't need any further incentives to frustrate the Johnson peace talks?

The sensible rule ought to be that when a substantial attempt is made by a candidate to procure the presidency by corrupt means, we may presume that he at least thought this would make a difference in the outcome, and thus we should resolve any doubts as to the effects of his efforts against him. Yet we must confine the operation of such a rule to truly substantial constitutional crimes, lest we ensnare every successful campaign in an unending postmortem in search of nonconstitutional misdeeds.

On this rule, the president could not be impeached for insider trading in securities, or for a narcotics violation if these occurred before he entered the White House. Doubtless there are middle cases that may or may not provide grounds for impeachment, such as a conspiracy to disturb the course of justice by promising pardons to win political support of their beneficiaries (which may amount to bribery) or concocting tax fraud schemes. These crimes would affect government operations, but unless the president takes some official act once he is in office, they do not in themselves amount to the constitutional crimes envisaged by our Framers and ratifiers.

This rule of construction also avoids an otherwise absurd conundrum: conspiracy with agents of a foreign state is not a problem before an election because there is no crime of electoral collusion on the federal statute books, but the obstruction of an investigation after an election also poses no problem for the conspirator because although it is a crime, a sitting president cannot be prosecuted and could thus serve out his term.

Seven Fallacies

Though much has changed in the practices of the US government and in the expectations of the public since 1974, much abides. From the very beginning of our life as a republic under a constitution ratified by our people, there have been six fundamental methods taken from English common law by means of which the Constitution has been applied. These six forms of argument—history, text, structure, doctrine, prudence, and ethos—are sometimes called "modalities," the philosophical term for the ways in which a proposition is determined to be true. In the constitutional law of the Unites States these six modalities determine whether a proposition of constitutional law is deemed to be true—whether the assertion of a particular constitutional principle accurately states the law. Together these six archetypal forms of argument compose the standard model by which judges, lawyers, officials, and citizens determine the law of the Constitution.

Indeed, that is the point of this book: impeachment is a matter of constitutional *law* and for this reason Charles Black's analysis remains as potent today as when it was written, despite the changes in American political society. One of these modalities—doctrine, or precedent—is applied according to the rule that the latest in time by the most authoritative source is dispositive. Thus the increased aggressiveness shown by the House in 1999 is now part of our law as to what the House may lawfully deem an impeachable offense. Another of the modalities—prudence, or the calculation of cost and benefits—also applies to a present context that is constantly shifting as the country's social, political, and economic situation changes. The public's demand for influence on events, effectuated by polling or social media, for example, and the media's demand for greater transparency in government, reflected in the deplorable anonymous release of confidential grand jury information, are as much the drivers of this change as they are its manifestations.

Case law and political calculation, however, are not the only forms of legitimate constitutional argument. Thus there are counter pressures to recent developments to be found in the *Federalist Papers* (history); in Black's lucid technical mastery of the ways in which the terms of a legal document are construed, like the rule of *eiusdem generis* (text); in the basic, though always contested, relations between a Congress that may not remove the president merely because a majority of its members have lost confidence in the administration, and the president who may not abuse his powers simply because he is unable to work the machinery of legislation effectively (structure); and in the tradition of the rule of law that is supreme over politics where constitutional rules are to be applied (ethos). These modalities are just as potent as doctrine and prudence, perhaps even more so when we are searching for firmer ground as the earth moves beneath our feet.

Moreover, even recent doctrine by an authoritative tribunal like the US Supreme Court can be wrong because the court's reasoning is found to be flawed. As a doctrinal matter, the limitation of *Bush* v. *Gore* to its own facts is a fatal admission of its vacuity as a precedent, and the Supreme Court has never relied on the case since it was handed down. Or the decision may remain contested because the various modalities point to different holdings. Even the unanimous holding in *Clinton* v. *Jones* will not save it from ridicule because of its prudentially naïve dismissal of the impact of a civil suit on the presidency. These observations may sound like technical matters, or subjects more fit for a treatise on jurisprudence than a handbook on the methods of impeachment, but they go to the heart of Black's book: impeachment is a matter of decision according to law, and there are some decisions we can make—according to the law of the Constitution—that will guide us even in terrain where the law is currently undecided. There are also some propositions of constitutional law that are demonstrably false and can be shown to be so. It might be well to dispose of them before we proceed to the application of constitutional law to our contemporary predicaments.

I've chosen seven of the most seductive of these fallacies (some constitutional scholars call them "myths"). Clearing them away will help us see the matter of impeachment more perspicuously. That some are widely and tenaciously held does not validate them, but is rather an implicit criticism of law professors and journalists whose job it is to inform and educate the public. That many people believe them is, while troubling, not dispositive; as the saying goes, ten times zero is still zero.

These fallacies are:

1. Impeachment is a political question, not a legal one.
2. The grounds for impeachment are whatever the House of Representatives determines them to be by voting a Bill of Impeachment and sending it to the Senate.
3. A criminal act by the president is an essential predicate to impeachment.
4. Any serious criminal act by the president is grounds for impeachment.
5. Congress cannot remove a president via impeachment for exercising or declining to exercise authorities that are constitutionally committed to the president's discretion.

6. Acts authorized by Congress cannot provide a predicate for the impeachment of the president who carries out these acts.

7. What constitutes a "high Crime or Misdemeanor" does not vary with the office of the person being impeached.

Sometimes these fallacies interlock. A person who thinks impeachment is a political, not a legal, matter may be inclined to believe that customary legal determinations like the assessment of motive or state of mind have no place in an impeachment inquiry, and therefore she may also accept the fallacy that a president cannot be impeached for his discretionary acts, whatever his purposes. Similarly, believing that impeachment is a political rather than a legal act gives grounds for concluding that an impeachable offense is whatever the House claims it is.

One fallacy may also share an erroneous assumption with another. If you think impeachment is fundamentally a response to the commission of an ordinary crime, not a constitutional crime, you may be more likely to conclude that impeachable offenses must be found in Title 18, "Crimes and Criminal Procedure," of the United States Code, and that Title 18 offenses provide a sufficient basis for impeachment.

The reason these fallacies endure is simply that their perpetrators haven't bothered to apply the legal methods to correctly assess them, perhaps because they don't ultimately believe impeachment *is* a matter of law and indeed may not believe that there is anything we can call "law" that is not politics. To someone taking this position, it may be unpersuasive to retort that that belief is incompatible with the US Constitution, which places law above political action in Article VI (among other places), because to such a skeptic the Constitution itself was little more than a snare for the gullible. But if that is the case, why bother with impeachment? Why not just march to the White House and arrest the president? And why should the president, who actually has armed forces at his command, sit still for an impeachment proceeding if not out of deference to the rule of law? Such views lead inevitably to violence and authoritarianism. Once law has been swept away, there remains no restraint on the competition for power. That these views are often urged by the advocates for the people who would be most vulnerable in the face of such violence is merely an irony.

Fallacy 1: Impeachment Is a Political Question, Not a Legal One

John Tyler, a former Democrat from Virginia, was added to the Whig ticket headed by William Henry Harrison in 1839. After succeeding to the presidency upon Harrison's death in 1841, he surprised many Whigs when he vetoed two important groups of Whig legislation on policy grounds (as opposed to constitutional grounds, which had hitherto generally been the basis for presidential vetoes). On July 12, 1842, an impeachment resolution was introduced in the House and a House select committee, headed by former president John Quincy Adams, was formed to consider the issue. Though Adams was a harsh critic of Tyler's and appears to have been persuaded of the necessity of eventual impeachment, he refused to press for the adoption of an impeachment resolution on the grounds that it would have been defeated in the Senate. This is the first example of an impeachment attempt against a president, and it appears to have been resolved on political rather than legal grounds. What constitutional support is there for such a resolution, that is, the decision on political grounds not to go forward with an otherwise valid case for impeachment?

First, the determinations to indict and to convict are made by two political bodies, not by the courts. Second, as a matter of recent precedent, there is ample evidence that most commentators in the

Congress and the media today assume that the impeachment question is "more political than legal," though the basis for this belief is rarely stated. Third, the passage of the Seventeenth Amendment, which took the selection of senators out of the hands of state legislatures and gave it directly to the voters, has suggested to some that for the Senate to resolve an impeachment indictment by the House on legal rather than political grounds would create a "counter-majoritarian difficulty"—meaning that it would risk thwarting the will of the popular majority. Fourth, and possibly most influential, is the idea that law is just politics anyway, and appeals to constitutional legal standards are little more than a charade, a cover for the reliance on political calculation. As a prominent constitutional lawyer put it in the *New York Times* in 2013,

> Law is just politics by a different name, and most Supreme Court justices are result-oriented, and choose legal theories (originalism, judicial activism and the like) as window dressing while they go where they want to go. Although these illusory labels can be treated as serious methodologies and may be of interest to law professors, the American legal system [is] just another part of government neither higher nor lower than the other two branches, and one that must be muscled.

Well, if that is true of the judicial system, what hope is there for the Congress when its members are called upon to act as judges and jurors? Finally, there is the Clinton precedent, which suggests that the acquittal of the president, on charges whose legal grounds were admittedly slight, was ultimately determined by his popularity with the public, which itself was based on factors that could scarcely be called *legal*.

Against the view that impeachment is principally or wholly a political matter is an important exchange at the Constitutional Convention—even though this exchange is frequently misconstrued to provide support for the claim that impeachment is not a legal matter. This exchange occurred when George Mason objected to limiting the grounds for impeachment to bribery and treason—the original formulation. He proposed adding the term "maladministration" which appeared in six of the thirteen state constitutions as a ground for impeachment, including that of Mason's own state of Virginia. After James Madison objected to the vagueness of "maladministration," Mason substituted "high Crimes and Misdemeanors." This phrase is defined in Blackstone's *Commentaries on the Laws of England*— a book the Framers knew well—as including, among other things, maladministration, and so quite a few persons have concluded that, at least to this extent, there is a permissible political basis for impeachment. In fact, the reason Madison gave for his objection to this term was that it would make the presidency equivalent to "a tenure during the pleasure of the Senate." But if the House may not impeach a president on grounds so general that they amount to his service at the mere consent of the Senate (as, for example, a prime minister can be removed by failing to win a vote of confidence in Parliament), then mere political grounds for impeachment cannot be the mandate of the Constitution.

Moreover, if the language is in some contexts open to competing constructions, there is one thing the text does not provide. As Akhil Amar has astringently noted, "The Constitution does not say that a president may be ousted when half the House and two-thirds of the Senate want him out."

In addition to these historical and textual arguments, there is the powerful precedent that since 1789, only nineteen federal officials have been impeached by the House, and of these only eight have been convicted by the Senate. Of the eight persons impeached and convicted, all were judges, and none were indicted on political grounds. In the same period, only two presidents—Andrew

Johnson and Bill Clinton—were tried by the Senate, and neither was found guilty. As Jane Chong observes, for "35% of our history, a US president has coexisted with a House controlled by the opposing party (that's 80 of the past 228 years since the start of the Washington administration). . . . [O]nly two presidents have suffered the disgrace of impeachment. Those two . . . were Democrats who were each ultimately acquitted by a Republican-controlled Senate." If the grounds for impeachment were political, one would expect it to be used more often for partisan reasons.

Finally, a passage from the *Federalist Papers*, often quoted out of context, appears to support the conclusion that impeachment is a political matter but actually does no such thing. This is the observation by Alexander Hamilton in *Federalist* #65 that "the subjects of [impeachments] are of a nature which may with peculiar propriety be denominated POLITICAL, as they relate chiefly to injuries done immediately to the society itself."

Read in context, however, Hamilton's reflection has the opposite import to that for which it is so often cited. In #65, Hamilton is at pains to show that the Senate can act in "their judicial character as a court for the trial of impeachments." Indeed he introduces the paper by saying that he will conclude his discussion "with a view of the judicial character of the Senate." A bit defensively, he continues,

> [A] well constituted court for the trial of impeachments is an object not more to be desired than difficult to be obtained in a government wholly elective. . . . The prosecution of them, for this reason, will seldom fail to agitate the passions of the whole community and to divide into parties more or less friendly or inimical to the accused. In many cases it will connect itself with pre-existing factions and will enlist all their animosities, partialities, influence and interest on one side or on the other; and in such cases there will always be the greatest danger that the decision will be regulated more by the comparative strength of the parties, than by the real demonstrations of innocence or guilt.

The entire essay is an attempt to show that the Senate can *overcome* its political nature as an elected body—chosen at the time by the members of the state legislatures—and act as a proper "court for the trial of impeachments." That is why Hamilton goes to great lengths to show that the Supreme Court is an inappropriate alternative—since it could be involved in subsequent criminal proceedings against the impeached president—and thus cannot substitute for the Senate.

Yet Justice Samuel Chase and President Andrew Johnson were impeached on political grounds—and they were cases of "first impression," that is, they were without precedent. What are we to make of this?

I think the resolution lies in differentiating the roles of the House and Senate. While the grounds for impeachment must be legal in nature, the decision whether to bring a Bill of Impeachment lies within the political discretion of the House, as John Quincy Adams urged. This is an extension of the analogy of the House proceedings to those of a grand jury, before which prosecutors have considerable leeway in determining what charges to press and which to decline to prosecute. The Senate, by contrast, sits as a law court: its proceedings are convened and presided over by the chief justice of the Supreme Court. More importantly, unlike the members of the House, senators take a special oath in addition to the oath of office that commands their fidelity to the Constitution. This second oath binds each member of the Senate to swear to "do impartial justice, according to the Constitution and laws: So help me God."

Fallacy 2: The Grounds for Impeachment Are Whatever the House Determines Them to Be

In 1968, President Lyndon Johnson nominated an associate justice to be chief justice of the Supreme Court to fill the vacancy created by the retirement of Earl Warren. In an effort to block this appointment, ethical charges were made against the nominee, Abe Fortas, that were sufficient to hold over the vacancy until after the election of Richard Nixon. This maneuver set in train a series of events, including the nomination and rejection of a capable appeals court judge, Clement Haynesworth, and then the rejection of his replacement, Harold Carswell, on grounds that infuriated partisans of the nominees. In the maelstrom of those confirmation fights, the Republican minority leader of the House, Gerald Ford, bruited the idea of impeaching the most liberal member of the court, William O. Douglas. It has been suggested that Ford thought a threatened impeachment could be a bargaining chip to be traded to the Democrats to get them to abandon their opposition to the Nixon nominees.

To preempt the creation of a select committee, which would divert jurisdiction from the Judiciary Committee, the Democratic chairman of that committee contrived to have a resolution of impeachment introduced against Douglas for "[h]igh crimes and misdemeanors and misbehavior in office." Ford, perhaps in frustration at this maneuver, spoke on April 15, 1970, to demand action by the Judiciary Committee. As to whether Douglas's alleged wrongs provided a sufficient basis for impeachment, Ford stated that "the only honest answer is that an impeachable offense is whatever a majority of the House of Representatives considers [it] to be at a given moment in history."

In his speech, Ford leveled five major charges against Douglas:

- Douglas had improperly failed to disqualify himself from the obscenity cases of a publisher who had paid him $350 for an article on folk singing that appeared in one of the publisher's magazines;
- Douglas's book, *Points of Rebellion*, violated standards of good behavior and was "an inflammatory volume";

- *Evergreen* magazine, which had published an excerpt from *Points of Rebellion*, also printed pornography;
- Douglas had a relationship with a private foundation that had paid him a director's fee (a similar arrangement with a nonprofit foundation had been the basis for charges against Fortas);
- the Center for the Study of Democratic Institutions, of which Douglas was chairman, was a "leftish" organization and a focal point for militant student unrest.

Ultimately, the Judiciary Committee refused to support Douglas's removal, and the midterm elections, in which the Democrats gained seats, and Ford's own lack of enthusiasm for the project caused the impeachment effort to fade away. But Ford's off-the-cuff remark that the grounds for impeachment are "whatever a majority of the House . . . considers [it] to be at a given moment" is apparently imperishable. What support is there for this widely held view?

There seems to be only one argument in support of Ford's claim. Because the decision to impeach is not reviewable by a court, any vote to impeach must go unexamined—it is argued—even if it is based on political or even personal animus. A Bill of Impeachment that dispensed with valid legal charges altogether would nevertheless be referred to the Senate for a trial, if the bill was approved by a House majority.

Perhaps nowhere than in reply to this insidious argument is there greater salience to Charles Black's words in this book that "we have to divest ourselves of the common misconception that constitutionality is discussable or determinable only in the courts." A corollary to this widely credited but nonetheless destructive misconception seems to be that outside the process of litigation in the courts, no government actor is bound by law. On the contrary, using the modalities of constitutional argument I have described earlier, it is possible for government officials—and the public and the media that assess their actions—to determine the legality of those acts and their constitutionality. In fact I would go further: it is incumbent upon the office holders and citizens of a democratic republic to do so.

Consider for a moment some of the objections to Congressman Ford's maxim. If it were true, then the House could impeach a federal official on account of her religious beliefs, despite the explicit provision of Article VI that "no religious Test shall ever be required as a Qualification to any Office or public Trust under the United States." Moreover, members of the judiciary would hold their posts at the pleasure of the Congress, in defiance of the system of sequenced and linked powers of the tripartite structure of the federal government. And as we have seen, Ford's rule would contradict the intention of the Framers and ratifiers that the basis for impeachment and removal from office be founded on evidence of bribery, treason, or similar offenses against the constitutional viability of the State.

What could possibly be meant by the requirement that Congress is bound by its oath to uphold the Constitution, if this applies only in adjudicated cases? Could the House attach a bill of attainder (a legislative act declaring a specific person guilty without trial) to the impeachment resolution forwarded to the Senate? Could it violate the prohibition on *ex post facto* laws by inventing a new high crime and misdemeanor—such as serving on the board of a "leftish" think tank—that few reasonable people would have anticipated would constitute grounds for removal by impeachment?

These points are so obvious that I must assume that they have not been overlooked by the advocates for Ford's dictum. Perhaps what these advocates really believe is that a majority of the members of the House of Representatives are prepared to lie about the true basis of their votes. But even if this were the case, it is not as damaging as Ford's claim that they needn't bother to do so.

Fallacy 3: A Criminal Act by the President Is an Essential Predicate to His Impeachment

Since 1936, virtually all successful judicial impeachments have involved criminal behavior, but that is hardly dispositive of the question whether the same standard should be applied to the president. Although the text is identical, the standards for impeachment of the president might well be unique because the *constitutional crimes* that can be committed by a president are unique. Moreover, the removal of the president reverses a national election (in most cases) and thus is a far graver step in a democracy than the removal of a single member of the judiciary.

Ironically, it may be this fact of uniqueness, the sense that a grave, historic step is being taken, that has intimidated members of the House, who may then wish to defend themselves against charges of having acted arbitrarily by relying on the explicit certainties of federal or state criminal codes. For example, one of the most constitutionally consequential charges against Richard Nixon was his use of the impoundment power—or "rescission"—as a super veto that could not be overridden. Instead of rescinding expenditures of funds appropriated and authorized by Congress owing to changed circumstances, as had been the practice since Jefferson, Nixon simply refused to spend the funds when appropriations were passed by the Congress over his veto. This is a constitutional crime that only the president can commit; it is unlikely to be in the statute books. Not only does it defy the Supreme Court's holding in the line item veto case, it takes that maneuver one step further by creating a veto that cannot be overridden. Had succeeding presidents emulated Nixon, impoundment would have unilaterally changed the allocation of powers created by Articles I and II. Nevertheless, all of the charges against Nixon adopted by the House were also common crimes. The House managers of the case against Bill Clinton were also anxious to stress the criminal aspect of the perjury charges leveled against him; they refused to include the abuse of power allegations recommended to them by the independent counsel.

The erroneous assumption that commission of a crime is an essential predicate for impeachment altered the course of the select committee to investigate the Iran-Contra affair. Democrats in the House who were anxious to impeach President Reagan felt compelled to demonstrate that he had been aware of the transfer of funds from the sale of missiles by Israel to Iran into accounts used to fund the Contra insurgency in Nicaragua, and thus that he had committed the common crime of misappropriation. Given President Reagan's management style, this was a difficult assignment, but, far more importantly, the effort to do so diverted the investigation away from the more consequential *constitutional* crime committed by the president when he set up a private covert action agency, run by the government but funded from private funds, including those from foreign countries.

Yet requiring investigators to show that a common crime has been committed may be useful as a check on hyperpartisanship in the impeachment process. Charles Black wrote that we "feel more comfortable when dealing with conduct clearly criminal in the ordinary sense, for as one gets further from that area it becomes progressively more difficult to be certain, as to any particular offense, that it is impeachable." But if this clarity and avoidance of partisan behavior provide prudential reasons for such a requirement, the Clinton impeachment does not support this surmise. All of the charges forwarded to the Senate alleged crimes, but the actual vote in the House fell almost strictly along partisan lines.

One need only consider a few hypothetical cases to realize how inadequate such a requirement would be for impeachment. What if the president required that all cabinet members affirm their belief in the divinity of Christ? Or that he devolved to his personal financial adviser classified intelligence about upcoming decisions of the Federal Reserve? Because the president can declassify any material he wishes, there is nothing *per se* illegal about this. What if the president announced that under no circumstances would he respond to the invocation of NATO's Article 5, which calls upon the signatories to the North Atlantic Treaty to aid each other when they are attacked? Or suspended habeas corpus after Congress had refused to do so and while Congress was in session? Suppose a candidate for the presidency conspired with foreign intelligence agencies to provide him with sophisticated data analytics in order that they could more effectively assist his campaign. This may or may not be a crime, depending on whether information from a foreign government amounts to the "giving of something of value" to the campaign, but it can scarcely be doubted that it is a high crime in the circumstances of a presidential election. As Black wrote after giving his own hypotheticals, "the limitation of impeachable offenses to those offenses made generally criminal by statute is unwarranted—even absurd."

This conclusion accords with James Wilson's observation that "our President . . . is amenable to [the laws] in his private character as a citizen, and in his public character by impeachment." It is also consistent with Justice Joseph Story's conclusion that the harms to be reached by impeachment are those "offensive acts which do not properly belong to the judicial character in the ordinary administration of justice, and are far removed from the reach of municipal jurisprudence."

Fallacy 4: Any Serious Criminal Act by the President Is Grounds for His Impeachment

Perhaps because bribery and treason are crimes, some have inferred that any crime could serve as the basis for impeachment of the president. This view is inconsistent, however, with the notion of a "high crime." Bribing a maître d' to get a good table at a restaurant might excite an overzealous prosecutor, but it could scarcely serve as a predicate for action by the House to remove a president. Like treason, the impeachable offense of bribery—like other impeachable offenses that are also common crimes—must be an act that actually threatens the constitutional stability and security of the State.

Here we have, fortunately, an important precedent, though not one decided by a court. As Chief Justice Rehnquist wrote in his own study of impeachment, *Grand Inquests*: "the impeachment acquittals of Justice Chase and President Johnson [were] 'cases' decided not by the courts but by the United States Senate."

Aaron Burr, vice-president during Jefferson's first term, killed Alexander Hamilton in a duel on July 11, 1804. There is some dispute as to whether Hamilton fired into the air before being shot in the spleen and liver by Burr, but there is no doubt that dueling was illegal both in New York, where both men were residents and where Hamilton was taken to die, and in New Jersey, where the duel took place. For the killing, Burr was indicted in both jurisdictions. (In New York, dueling was a capital offense.)

Yet after first fleeing to South Carolina, Burr returned to Washington to complete his term as vice-president. Not only was he not impeached by a Congress controlled by the president, who despised him, but in his role as vice-president, he subsequently presided over the first impeachment, against the Federalist judge Samuel Chase, and was given high marks for his judicial temperament and impartiality.

When construing the Constitution on the grounds of historical argument, we give great weight to the actions of the first few Congresses and presidents because they were familiar with the understandings on the basis of which our people ratified the governing document. It is obviously true, with respect to judges, that any serious crime is a sufficient predicate for bringing a Bill of Impeachment; as we have seen, nine members of the judiciary have been impeached, mainly on the basis of having committed common crimes. But what about Burr? Whether we say that the vice-president stands with the president, perhaps because he too is elected by the entire nation, or whether we place him on some lesser pedestal nearer the judges, the fact that Burr was not impeached suggests that at the very least a president cannot be lawfully impeached for the commission of an ordinary crime—even murder. Charles Black found it inconceivable that "a president who had committed murder could not be removed by impeachment." He came to this conclusion because such a crime "would so stain a president as to make his continuance in office dangerous to public order. . . . We could punish a traitorous or corrupt president after his term expired; we *remove* him principally because we fear he . . . is not thinkable as a national leader."

What looks like a paradoxical precedent can actually be harmonized with the standards we have thus far derived. An impeachable offense is one that puts the Constitution in jeopardy. This act might also be a common crime, but the reason we impeach is not to punish common crimes. In the Burr case, the insignificant role of the vice-president in that period, the nearness of his term's end, perhaps even the alienation between Burr and Jefferson all militated against impeachment.

This analysis also explains Congress's rough treatment of the judges. It wasn't simply because they had committed common crimes that they were impeached and removed from office. Rather it was because having committed a common crime, they had undermined their own ability to serve in the judiciary where they must assess and render judgment on the common crimes of others.

Perhaps this is the place to reaffirm Black's position that a serving president must be impeached before he or she can be indicted and tried for an ordinary crime. This point is made repeatedly in the *Federalist Papers*. In #65, Hamilton observes that

> the punishment which may be the consequence of conviction upon impeachment is not to terminate the chastisement of the offender. *After* having been sentenced to perpetual ostracism from the esteem and confidence and honors and emoluments of his country, he will still be liable to prosecution and punishment in the ordinary course of law.

This point is made again in *Papers* #69 and #77, which assert that the president could not be prosecuted as a criminal until he had left office, a point confirmed in the first Congress by both Oliver Ellsworth and Vice-President John Adams.

Moreover, as a prudential matter this surely cannot be an open question. Does anyone really think, in a country where common crimes are usually brought before state grand juries by state prosecutors, that it is feasible to subject the president—and thus the country—to every district attorney with a reckless mania for self-promotion? Have we forgotten Jim Garrison already?

Thus the question, which I will take up in the next chapter, whether a president's obstruction of the operations of the Department of Justice must track the requirements of the criminal statutes that prohibit the obstruction of justice in order to serve as the basis for impeachment, misses the point. As Black observed, the constitutional significance of the fact that an impeachable offense may share elements with a common crime is only that judges and executive officials are put on notice of the impropriety of certain acts.

In any case, we no longer have to make this choice because the Twenty-Fifth Amendment allows us a way out. If a crime is sufficiently shaming as to make the president "not thinkable as a national leader," we may presume that the vice-president and a majority of the principal officers of the executive branch (or some other body that Congress has designated) have grounds to declare that the president is unable to discharge the powers and duties of his office. Should the president resist, Congress must determine whether the president is fit to continue in office. It may transfer his powers to the vice-president by a two-thirds vote of both houses.

Fallacy 5: Congress Cannot Remove a President for Exercising Authorities That Are Constitutionally Committed to His Discretion

Certain authorities are granted by Congress to the president, for instance by the Authorization for the Use of Military Force after 9/11. In the next chapter I will discuss whether Congress can impeach a president who acts pursuant to such powers in the absence of countervailing statutes. But other powers are granted directly to the president by the Constitution, including those accorded to him as head of the executive departments and thus as chief law enforcement officer, the pardon power, and authority over the armed forces as commander in chief. Can Congress impeach a president for acts committed pursuant to power that is exclusively his?

Interestingly, in light of the importance of the early Congresses, the House in the first session of the first Congress discussed impeachment extensively. The issue was whether the president had to return to the Congress for permission to remove the head of an executive department appointed by him and confirmed by the Senate. If a cabinet appointment required the participation of the Senate, did dismissal also require Senate action?

On the floor of the House, James Madison argued that the Constitution vested the power of removal exclusively in the president. He went on to say that this was "absolutely necessary" because "it will make him in a peculiar manner, responsible for [their] conduct." This responsibility, Madison argued, would "subject [the president] to impeachment himself, if he suffers them to perpetrate with impunity High crimes or misdemeanors against the United States, or neglects to superintend their conduct, so as to check their excesses."

This might seem a surprising position to those who hold the erroneous view that the president has constitutional immunity from impeachment for his discretionary exercise of powers granted him exclusively by the Constitution. Those enticed by this fallacy draw support—if wrongly—from the constitutional crisis that led to the impeachment of Andrew Johnson. By adopting the Tenure of Office Act, Congress sought to require President Johnson to seek senatorial consent before removing his secretary of war. Johnson, citing the "power and authority vested in the President by the Constitution," nevertheless removed Edwin Stanton, a Lincoln appointee, without seeking or obtaining the Senate's consent. The House cited this action as grounds for Johnson's impeachment. The first Article of Impeachment claimed that Johnson was "unmindful . . . [when he issued an order] for the removal of Edwin M. Stanton" of the Constitution's requirement that the laws be faithfully executed. The general consensus today, ratified by the Supreme Court in *Myers* v. *United States,* is that Madison and Johnson were right. The president does not have to return to the Senate to remove an executive official who was confirmed by that body. Does this mean that the power specifically allocated to the president grants him a kind of constitutional immunity to impeachment for the exercise of that power?

It has been claimed, for example, that the president cannot be impeached for acts that in another's hands would amount to obstruction of justice—for example, trying to dissuade the director of the FBI or the attorney general from pursuing a particular criminal investigation—because the president has the exclusive authority to direct the officials of the Justice Department to pursue prosecutions. As a lawyer for the president pithily put it, "he cannot obstruct himself."

Or can the president be impeached for according recognition to the government of a foreign state? It seems obvious that the Congress could not require the president to recognize a particular foreign state; that power is his exclusively. How, then, could his exercise of such a power be the basis for impeachment? How, in other words, can the Congress coerce the president via impeachment to take steps that it would be unconstitutional for the Congress to require by statute?

These questions are confused by failing to differentiate between the exercise of a lawful power, and the unlawful exercise of such a power. For example, the president could clearly be impeached were he to take bribes from a foreign state in exchange for recognition. The grounds for impeachment lie not in the exercise of the power *per se* but in its corrupt exercise. In Andrew Johnson's case, the claim wasn't so much that the president had behaved improperly in exercising his constitutional powers; on the contrary, those very constitutional powers were at issue. If Johnson's claim to have the exclusive right to dismiss executive officials was correct, then to hold otherwise would mean that the command to "take care that the laws be faithfully executed" included executing laws that were unconstitutional—that is, laws that were not US law.

But Johnson's case, like the purchase of a pardon or the treasonous exercise of the president's power as commander in chief, is easy. What if a foreign power somehow induced the president to order US-led forces in Syria to stand aside when Kurdish forces allied with the United States were attacked? What if the president, instead of ordering the Department of Justice to stop investigating the White House, instead used his power over the CIA to direct the Agency to mislead DOJ investigators? Let's go back to Madison's argument for giving the president exclusive authority in the first place. Madison argued that such authority would ensure the president's impeachment if he permitted misconduct. This is in sympathy with James Wilson's argument that the virtue of locating executive authority in one person was that it would ensure his accountability. That the president is responsible for the actions of executive officials makes him responsible when these actions are unlawful, and makes him impeachable when they are constitutional crimes. This leads us to conclude that the constitutional crimes he directs others to commit can provide the basis for his impeachment.

Fallacy 6: Acts Authorized by Congress Cannot Provide a Predicate for the Impeachment of the President Who Carries Out These Acts

A slightly different point from Wilson's and Madison's was raised by Elbridge Gerry during the colloquy quoted in the previous section concerning the impeachability of the president for his discretionary acts. Gerry said that a president could not be impeached when he was "doing an act which the Legislature has submitted to his discretion"—that is, when the president's power to perform the act is delegated by statute rather than exclusively assigned to the executive by the Constitution. This raises the question of whether Congress is estopped (prevented by its own acts) from pursuing an impeachment in such circumstances. Suppose, having been fully informed by the executive, Congress provided funds for a paramilitary covert action that went horribly wrong. Surely the president could not be impeached for his oversight of such an enterprise on the grounds that the undertaking was too risky.

Similarly, it has been argued that a president's violations of the Emoluments Clause could readily be rebuffed by congressional legislation against conflicts of interest. Does it make sense to use the drastic weapon of impeachment when the Congress has refused the less consequential but equally effective method of statutory action? Could the president argue that congressional inaction—and implicit congressional complicity in the example above—can mislead the president, even entrap him? This may be what Charles Black had in mind when he wrote that the impeachment of Richard Nixon for secret military operations in Cambodia, of which the leaders of the Congress were well aware and to which they had not objected, was close to the line.

But a rule that estopped Congress from impeaching in such circumstances would run afoul of one of the most basic precepts of the US Constitution: one Congress cannot bind another to its decisions. One often hears politicians promise that a particular statute will force Congress to live within certain limits, such as a revenue cap at a certain percentage of GDP. Apart from the moral suasion and the political reaction that might befall a transgressor, there is no reason this should be true. A Congress cannot even bind itself, and it can always repeal earlier action using the same procedures by which the earlier legislation was adopted. A rule that prevented impeachment owing to prior acts of congressional duplicity or even encouragement by the Congress would amount to an unconstitutional, if ineffectual, restraint on future action by the Congress.

Furthermore, impeachment and legislation, even when directed toward the same object—to prevent corruption in the case of emoluments—are far different modes of action. Statutory action has a policy purpose, correcting a past wrong or deterring a future one; impeachment is a "National Inquest," as Hamilton termed it, that exposes constitutional crimes and has no particular policy purpose other than protecting the State. A rule that estopped congressional action would waive the public's right to the exposure of wrongdoing that comes with the trial (and the defense against such charges on the grounds that the president has been unjustly accused).

The rule in such circumstances ought to be: Congress may impeach on grounds that would be impeachable, regardless of any other congressional acts.

Fallacy 7: What Constitutes a "high Crime or Misdemeanor" Does Not Vary with the Office of the Person Being Impeached

The study of constitutional law should enable the student to master all the conventional forms of American constitutional argument—text, history, structure, prudence, ethos, and doctrine. That is because while all these forms usually cohere and reinforce each other—as, for example, they do in answering the important question of the legitimacy of judicial review—sometimes they do not.

Sometimes the text will be especially authoritative and can override the distant murmurs of history. Article I, section 6 of the Constitution refers to "Treason, Felony, and Breach of the Peace"; Article IV, section 2 speaks of "Treason, Felony, or other Crime." We know that in writing the Impeachment Clause, the Framers took the phrase "high Crimes and Misdemeanors" from British impeachment practice, yet we also know that this practice had become odious by the time the Americans drafted their Constitution, and little of the purpose of British impeachment—removing ministers of the Crown who were protected by the king—is relevant to the American government. A comparison of the three texts, however, shows us that whatever the Framers and ratifiers had in mind, "high Crimes and Misdemeanors" most likely did not mean common crimes like felonies or breaches of the peace.

Sometimes we will want ethos and structure to provide distinctions that the framework language of a Constitution does not. Nothing in the text of the Constitution specifically forbids a state from taxing the operations of the federal government. The notion, however, that a legislative body can tax only those persons who are represented in that body—or who seek its protection—is a fundamental principle of our constitutional ethos and the structure of federalism. The same sort of analysis applies to the confirmation of judges and cabinet members: the text makes no distinction between them, but lifetime appointment to a coordinate branch of government demands much stricter scrutiny than the fulfillment of a president's judgment in choosing his subordinates.

This marshaling of the forms of argument helps us dismiss the suggestion that the standards for the impeachment of a president are the same as they are for judges and other civil officers. Here, too, the text makes no distinction, but as a structural matter, equal standards would be nonsensical. The grounds for the expulsion of the one person elected by the entire nation to preside over the executive cannot be the same as those for one member of the almost four-thousand-member federal judiciary. Unlike criminal proceedings, which are designed to treat all defendants alike regardless of their station, impeachment is not a criminal proceeding—that's why double jeopardy doesn't forbid the subsequent trial of an impeached official. Impeachment is the attack of one office on another; civilians cannot be impeached. Thus the relative responsibilities of the official to be impeached are automatically drawn into the question. The duties of the president—especially with respect to foreign and military affairs—make it obvious that the threats to the State posed by presidential misconduct are unique. The language of the text provides a floor, not a ceiling.

This is a profound structural difference, and it militates against the broader array of errors for which we would remove a judge, who is unelected. Discussion of impeachment in the *Federalist Papers*, our best resource for historical argument about the intentions behind the original, unamended text, stresses the unique responsibilities of the president and his unique vulnerabilities. Almost nothing is said of the other civil officers subject to impeachment, yet we can readily infer that the basis for removing judges and magistrates also arises from their unique responsibilities. Ambassadors are vulnerable to seduction by foreign interests; regulators to being co-opted by those they regulate; and judges, whose behavior in conducting court proceedings requires a reputation for probity, can be removed for arbitrariness or want of personal dignity.

Prudential values are also at stake. We wouldn't want to pause the nation's business to search for presidential peccadilloes; nor would we want to cripple the country's authority in foreign negotiations by casting doubt on the viability of "the chief organ of foreign relations" unless he posed some historic threat to our constitutional order.

This is further confirmed by doctrine. Although prosecutors in the House have repeatedly attempted to ensnare presidents in alleged wrongs having little to do with any official transgression—from Andrew Johnson to Bill Clinton—they have been uniformly rebuffed. The Senate has refused to convict on such charges, while evidencing no such compunction about charges against judges.

The impeaching House and the trying Senate derive their power from the consent of the governed, and it is a cardinal principle of our constitutional life that governments are created to protect the rights of the governed—including the right to have their consent manifested in the persons chosen to govern. That means protecting the electorate's choice of president, unless the very destruction of the protecting State and its constitutional norms is at stake. In this way too, the president is in a very different position from that of a federal magistrate or cabinet member.

CHAPTER 8

Particular Problems

In 1974, introducing his chapter entitled "Application to Particular Problems," Charles Black wrote:

> In what follows, I do not intend in any way to judge any real-life issue. Questions of exact fact and of evidence are always crucial, and it is not in any case my wish here to decide anything. But some questions are inevitably suggested by events, and can be dealt with tentatively.

In this similarly titled chapter, I intend to apply the analysis thus far outlined to some issues around impeachment that are on people's minds today but that did not preoccupy the public in 1974. This can be helpful by giving concrete form to our methods and also to indicate why and in what ways the context for impeachment has altered since then.

The principal changes in context that have brought these hitherto obscure questions to the fore are (1) new technologies of information, (2) new political norms of behavior that both drive and derive from our changing culture of governance, and (3) the emergence of political leaders whose habits reflect an entrepreneurial rather than a managerial or legal background.

Some of these new challenges test one's previous constitutional commitments, in my case, for example, to the unitary executive, that is, the idea that the president as chief executive has control over all the acts of the officials of the various departments. Similarly, Nixon's invocation of executive privilege tested Black's commitment to preventing the Congress from weakening the structural integrity of the presidency. Should one's constitutional sense of how things ought to be done—what is appropriate and well adapted to our constitutional system—change in a new era of political competition, or with new technologies for campaigning, or in light of unprecedented practices by candidates? A constitution is intended to endure for ages to come, and consequently to be adapted to the various crises of human affairs. But it is also meant to provide the methods for achieving legitimacy to those adaptations, and—except in the greatest crises—that means providing continuity with our legal traditions rather than chasing the curve balls thrown by novel and even apparently threatening developments.

Burglary

In May 1972, a team directed by the Nixon campaign broke into the Democratic National Committee (DNC) headquarters, located in the Watergate office complex. There they planted two listening devices and stole copies of confidential documents. When the telephone bugs failed to operate properly, the team reentered the Watergate on June 17 in order to photograph documents and to plant two new microphones in an office adjacent to that of DNC and campaign chairman Lawrence O'Brien. The burglars were arrested by police as they left the premises.

In March 2016, the email account of Hillary Clinton's campaign chair was hacked, and a vast trove of communications was stolen. In June and July, DCLeaks and WikiLeaks released emails taken from the Democratic National Committee. More were subsequently obtained by WikiLeaks and released in October and November 2016. Ultimately, more than 150,000 emails were published, stolen from more than a dozen Democrats.

Taken as a whole, it is remarkable how benign, though occasionally petty, and how earnest, though occasionally disenchanted, these emails are. But carefully culled, phrases and sentences can be made to seem more sinister, and these were picked up by American social media and US news organizations, some hostile to the Clinton campaign, and Russian troll farms to give the impression of a bigger story than the facts warranted. Classification labels like "Confidential" were pasted in to make the stolen documents more enticing to journalists. Juxtaposed in this way, it seems obvious that the Watergate break-ins of 1972 were a precursor for the electronic break-ins of 2016. Only the revolution in information technology, which made possible the vast change in scale and the relative immunity of the burglars, is different.

For our purposes, the question is what culpability is laid at a candidate's door if he uses the fruits of these thefts in the closing days of a presidential election and even publicly (and perhaps privately) encourages the thefts. For example, in New Hampshire the day before the general election, the Republican candidate said, "[My opponent] has shown contempt for the working people of this country. [In] WikiLeaks they have spoken horribly about Catholics and evangelicals and so many others. They got it all down, folks. WikiLeaks. WikiLeaks." And the day before in Iowa, "Just today we learned [my opponent] was sending highly classified information through her maid. WikiLeaks!" Four days before in Florida, "Out today, WikiLeaks just came out with a new one, it's just been shown that a rigged system with more collusion, possibly illegal, between the Department of Justice, [my opponent's] campaign, and the State Department."

Exploiting negative information about a political opponent, even if that information is the fruit of a burglary—as the WikiLeaks release clearly was—does not furnish grounds for an impeachment. In the WikiLeaks case, the information was enthusiastically picked up by the *New York Times* and other mainstream outlets, carefully dripping revelations on their front pages day by day, despite their editors' knowing the illegal provenance of the materials they were releasing. How could the House penalize a candidate for repeating—even exaggerating—information in the public domain? Where there is no evidence of a conspiracy between the campaign and the burglars, or no evidence that the candidate was aware of such a conspiracy, much less orchestrated it, there is no constitutional crime. Were the burglary commissioned or facilitated by the campaign's leadership, that might well serve as the basis for counts of impeachment. One might reasonably argue, in that case, that impeachment is the only equitable remedy, because the result of the election is the fruit of the crime. In that case, we simply cannot know what the true result of the voting would have been, because the election's outcome was perverted by unlawful acts.

But imagine a different hypothetical. Suppose such a burglary—a cyberburglary—were part of a pattern of long-standing efforts by a foreign power to ensnare and inculpate a private party by granting his enterprises favorable governmental rulings and advantageous loans, with the aim of acquiring influence by compromising an otherwise innocent party. We are on alert for this sort of thing in our domestic politics, but in *Federalist* #68, Hamilton observed that "cabal, intrigue, corruption might naturally have been expected to make their approaches from more than one quarter, but chiefly from the desire in foreign powers to gain an improper ascendant in our counsels." Then the indictment by the House and the fact-finding to be tried by the Senate would be a more complex undertaking.

The Senate would have to determine whether the president was influenced by such sympathetic support—including but not limited to the burglary, whether or not he was aware of the foreign state's intention.

There can be little doubt that the remedy for acting on such inducements would be impeachment. At the Philadelphia Convention in 1787, Gouverneur Morris explained why he changed his mind about the need for an impeachment provision in the Constitution: "[N]o one would say that we ought to expose ourselves to the danger of seeing the first magistrate in foreign pay without being able to guard against it by displacing him."

Bots

There is no longer any doubt that Russian agents distributed information through social media to networks and virtual communities: posting articles on false Facebook pages, deploying a battalion of trolls, directing tens of thousands of bots to simulate waves of reaction and aim them at susceptible opinion, and to retweet false information from fake sources. In a creative twist on "hybrid warfare," the Russians over many years have developed an increasing sophistication in the digitalization of disinformation.

US counterintelligence reports in March 2017 disclosed that the Russian government had used these tactics to influence key aides of members of Congress. Disinformation was broadcast on social media, which were then carefully monitored to see how the targets responded in an attempt to find those susceptible persons who might unwittingly support Russian objectives. The reports detailed how on August 7, 2016, a story was circulated that Hillary Clinton had Parkinson's disease. That story went viral in August and exploded after Clinton nearly fainted from pneumonia and dehydration in early September. Other false stories were circulated saying that Pope Francis had endorsed the Republican nominee and that Hillary Clinton had engineered the murder of a DNC staffer.

Counterintelligence officials have found evidence that during the campaign Russia targeted influential persons who would spread damaging stories fed to them. Russian operatives used algorithmic techniques to target the social media accounts of particular reporters, bought ads on Facebook to target propaganda at specific populations, and funded computer-mediated technologies and fake news outlets, which they targeted with increasing precision on voters in swing districts, notably in Michigan, Wisconsin, and Pennsylvania.

The campaign manager for the Republican nominee on August 14 cited an attack on the US base at Incirlik, Turkey—a bit of fake news that originated with Russia. The nominee himself at various times picked up misinformation from a *Sputnik* news agency site and legitimated it by repeating it to his followers. False information pushed by Russian fronts was repeated by the Republican nominee's team in campaign briefings; hacks and leaks by the Russians were synchronized with actions taken in the nominee's campaign. The campaign of the Republican nominee often picked up fake news items and false lines presented by the Russians, and the Russians would repeat false information that originated with his campaign. The exploitation of the WikiLeaks disclosures of thousands of hacked emails from the DNC and the leadership of the Clinton campaign was one part of this pattern.

The implications for the impeachment process depend on whether the nominee, later the president, was aware of these operations; if so, when did he become aware of them; and what, if anything, did he do to encourage them, collaborate with them, or help conceal them. These inquiries are analogous to Senator Howard

Baker's famous questions about President Nixon and the Watergate break-in: "What did he know, and when did he know it?"

Let's apply these questions to a hypothetical. Assume three groups of actors: FBI personnel, Republican campaign officials, and Russian intelligence agents. Suppose the campaign officials shuffle information between the two intelligence agencies—giving the FBI information obtained by the Russian agents (without identifying the source) about potentially unlawful activities conducted by the Democratic campaign, and also giving the Russian agents information from the FBI to assist the Russians' ongoing disinformation campaign about the Democrats. Suppose further that Russian agents possess incriminating information on the Democratic campaign, and have promised to release it in exchange for favorable policy positions in the Republican party platform—relief of sanctions against Russia and tacit acceptance of Russia's annexation of Crimea, for example. If these discussions occurred, it might well be that Republican campaign officials saw nothing wrong either with their participation in the WikiLeaks operation or with their collaboration with friendly agents in the FBI. Since all the leading media outlets had relished publishing WikiLeaks material, what is wrong with giving information about possible crimes to the FBI? Whether it shows an alarming naïveté on the part of the campaign or an equally alarming sophistication on the part of the Russians, it is easy to see how, step by step, campaign personnel could have been led to participate in these disinformation efforts. That this made the Republican campaign leadership into a kind of "cut-out," or insulating intermediary, for Russian intelligence does not mean that the candidate himself directed or even understood what was happening.

Given such a set of hypothetical facts, it is difficult to see how the candidate could, if elected, be found liable to impeachment absent definitive evidence that he directed his subordinates to conspire with agents of a hostile foreign power or proof of his promise to adopt the policy positions urged on him by those collaborating in the disinformation campaign. Moreover, it would be very hard to show that there was an exchange of promises. As we have seen countless times in our domestic politics, the recipient of assistance can always say, often credibly, that he would have taken the position desired by his patron anyway.

Whether or not these operations were undertaken in a conspiracy with a hostile foreign power, they do not amount to treason. The Framers, wary of the danger that this legal concept might be used as a political weapon, enshrined in the Constitution itself a highly restrictive and binding definition:

"Treason against the United States, shall consist only in levying War against them, or in adhering to their Enemies, giving them Aid and Comfort."

If we are not in a formal state of war with a hostile power—even if Russia is to be considered such a power—the giving of "Aid and Comfort" to that power in its campaign to defeat a US presidential candidate would not serve as a basis for a charge of treason.

Putting aside issues of evidence, as a matter of constitutional law, a conspiracy to pervert the course of a presidential election—whether by sophisticated technological means or simple vote stealing, and whether in league with a hostile foreign power or not—is an impeachable offense. That it may have occurred prior to the president's taking office does not matter. The legal basis for impeachment would be overwhelming.

The instructions of the *Federalist Papers* could not be clearer that impeachment is a punishment for a political crime. In a democratic republic, whose legitimacy depends upon frequent popular elections, there could scarcely be a more manifest example of such a crime. The constitutional language of "high Crimes," which refers to the damage done to the State's legitimacy when its officials are bribed or suborned by foreign enemies, confirms the seriousness with which the Framers viewed this matter. The structure of the federal government deploys the Congress—with its broad representational mandate—in a judicial function when it indicts, tries, and convicts a president; that this is appropriate for a constitutional crime seems obvious. As a matter of prudence, an illegitimately elected president could not expect the allegiance of his subordinates—some of whom would be subject to criminal process—or of the People. As Black put it, "Who would salute?" As an ethical matter, it would be intolerable to allow a president to profit by such a crime, just as we do not permit a murderer to collect the insurance on the deceased; it is an ancient maxim that one cannot benefit from one's crime (*commodum ex injuria sua nemo habere debet*). Finally, as a doctrinal matter, while there is no precise precedent, the Nixon impeachment suggests that tampering with the electoral process is *prima facie* a high crime or misdemeanor.

Obstruction

Whether or not a president was aware of foreign digitalized disinformation operations before they were exposed, if he attempted to impede valid government investigations of these activities in an effort to forestall their exposure and prosecution—for example, by directing subordinates to make false statements to DOJ investigators, or by offering various incentives to DOJ officials to end their investigations of those operations—these facts would be important to determine. It may well be that the Republican candidate and his senior team were unaware of any of the developments described in the previous section, or that they discounted reports of them; let's assume that. Yet at some point, the president-elect must have learned of these facts, even if he refused to believe that they affected the outcome of the election.

Many commentators at the time professed to be baffled as to what happened after the acting attorney general went to the White House to warn that the new national security advisor had been lying to the FBI about his contacts with the Russian ambassador and that the Russians were aware of this. Why was no action immediately taken? Didn't the president take these warnings seriously? Shouldn't he have been alarmed by the charge that his national security advisor might be vulnerable to Russian blackmail?

Putting to one side the much more serious issue of collaboration with Russia to manipulate the election, or a possible effort to cover up that collaboration, suppose that the following lay behind the events. The president-elect instructed his soon-to-be national security advisor to tell the Russian ambassador not to be too upset about the previous administration's sanctions against Russia because he planned to reverse them once he became president. The president-elect saw no problem with undermining the previous administration's policy—after all there would be a new president in a few weeks. Not until a *Washington Post* article appeared exposing these pre-inauguration contacts was the president forced to dismiss his agent.

In this hypothetical, the president would not be moved by the attorney general's warning; he knew his national security advisor couldn't be blackmailed with the threat of exposure to the president because there was nothing to expose. Nevertheless, the president may have begun to realize that pre-inauguration contacts with the Russians, while intended to be merely reassuring, had given the Russians a weapon to get their own way should they threaten the disclosure of these contacts to the public. Coupled with the collusion charges then beginning to surface, the possibility of such a disclosure might well have motivated the new president to make efforts to quell any investigation into the matter, including firing his own national security advisor.

Perhaps this hypothetical even helps us analyze other situations in which a president is grappling with a crisis of legitimacy that may be only partly of his making.

One sometimes neglected element in our construction of the impeachment term "bribery" is that, as Black put it, "bribery may mean the *taking* as well as the *giving* of a bribe." "Is it 'bribery,'" he asks, "to suggest to a federal judge, engaged in trying a case crucial to the executive branch, that the directorship of the Federal Bureau of Investigation might be available?" It all depends on the motive and intent of the president.

Imagine further that a president invited the FBI director to dinner at the White House, and in the course of their discussion the director asked whether he would be kept on, and the president said, "I'll think about it" and then immediately asked whether he was the subject of an FBI investigation. This might put the president on dangerous ground. The fact that he could simply order the FBI director to cease any such investigation does not alter the fact that offering an inducement to act—by, for example, suggesting that the director's future in his official position might hinge on his shutting down an investigation of the president—comes perilously close to offering a bribe. It is no defense to say that the appointment, unlike the secret payment, is made in public: the bribe is not the appointment, but the promise to appoint in exchange for the performance of an official act.

Suppose, then, the president expressed the hope that the FBI director would drop the investigation into the dismissed national security advisor (whose lying to federal officials about pre-inauguration contacts with the Russians may well have been done at the president's direction). In the context of the pending reappointment (or dismissal) of the director, this, too, could be construed as a quid pro quo. The fact that the president could have simply ordered the FBI to drop the investigation actually counts against him: it makes it appear that he was loath to give that order and was seeking some extra-constitutional way to bring about the same result. This construction is confirmed if the president has tried to get other agencies, like the National Security Agency and the office of the director of national intelligence, to interfere with the FBI. Because the investigation concerns the president's own conduct, these actions suggest that rather than taking care to see that the laws are faithfully enforced, he is, for self-serving and possibly even sinister motives, trying stealthily to derail their enforcement. Suppose, as well, we learned from a National Security Council memorandum of the president's conversation with Russian diplomats and that he told them, "I just fired the head of the FBI. I faced great pressure because of Russia. That's taken off."

It's worth recalling that Article 1, section 4 of the Articles of Impeachment against President Nixon accused him of "interfering or endeavouring to interfere with the conduct of investigations by the Department of Justice [and] the Federal Bureau of Investigation." From this we have another famous phrase of the era—"It's not the crime, it's the cover-up."

Legal commentators who think the key question is whether the president's actions violated Title 18 U.S.C. 73 miss the point. "Obstruction of justice" does not appear in the Constitution. Whether it can serve as a basis for an impeachment depends on whether the president's actions constitute the kind of wanton constitutional dereliction captured by the phrase "high Crimes and Misdemeanors," not on whether they conform to the prohibitions contained in a criminal statute. Attempting to distort an otherwise valid investigation of the executive by the Department of Justice and the FBI is a basis for impeachment that is affirmed by the precedent of Nixon's impeachment.

The standards of a criminal statute, which are supposed to be quite rigorous in our system, and which generally require *scienter,* or knowledge of wrongdoing, on the part of the defendant, cannot substitute for the standards of impeachment by the House and conviction by the Senate. The standards for impeachment need not depend upon the president's actual intent to commit a crime, constitutional or otherwise. The Framers repeatedly stated that the president could be impeached for the acts of his subordinates, whether or not he directed them in their misdeeds.

That doesn't mean that the president's motives are irrelevant, only that the inquiry for a statutory crime is not the same as for a constitutional crime. Once out of office, a president can always be prosecuted for his statutory violations, and if convicted, his conviction can be contested and appealed. But the damage done by undoing an election through an impeachment that depends on too many inferences from behavior that may have been innocent cannot be so easily remedied. Motives count, even if they need not be as specific as those demanded by the ordinary criminal processes.

Pardons

In September 1974, President Gerald Ford pardoned his predecessor Richard Nixon for all crimes that Nixon had "committed or may have committed or taken part in" with regard to the Watergate scandal. Although the *New York Times* editorial board proclaimed this a "profoundly unwise, divisive, and unjust act," most persons today looking back at that action—which clearly cost Ford the presidential election in 1976—see it as a decent, humane, and courageous step toward healing the nation and getting the administration back to the business of governing. It was just such purposes that were contemplated by the Framers, who in drafting the pardon power mixed mercy with a shrewd eye to repairing political division. As Hamilton wrote in *Federalist* #74, "Humanity and good policy conspire" in the pardon power. George Washington's pardon of the participants in the Whiskey Rebellion remains the paradigm.

Yet the increasingly degraded culture of American politics may someday present a novel set of possibilities: a cornered president may pardon his coconspirators, and even attempt to pardon himself. Such scenarios would have been unthinkable in the past.

Article II, section 2 of the Constitution provides that the president "shall have the Power to grant Reprieves and Pardons for offenses against the United States, except in cases of Impeachment." From this spare text we can draw several legal conclusions: (1) that the power is unlimited with respect to federal crimes but does not extend to federal civil actions, state crimes, or impeachments; and (2) that a pardon cannot extend to a future act, there being no "offense" to which a pardon may be applied. This reading was confirmed by a 1975 federal district court ruling that upheld the Ford pardon, citing an 1867 US Supreme Court decision during the administration of Andrew Johnson. We can also conclude (3) that apart from the explicit terms of the text, a pardon cannot prevent impeachment because impeachment is not a criminal process.

Does that mean, as some have written, that a president may not be impeached for exercising his "unlimited" power to pardon? It most certainly does not. To take the most obvious case, summoned up by Black, suppose that a pardon were procured through bribery, or that "the president granted a set of pardons to assist a foreign adversary in waging war against the United States." In these cases and in other clear examples—Black asks us to contemplate a president who announces a policy of granting pardons to all police who kill anyone in the line of duty in Washington, whatever the circumstances of the killing—the president could certainly be impeached, and following conviction, he could be indicted and tried (including as an accessory after the fact, that is, as someone who may not have been aware of the original plan to commit a crime but who facilitated escape).

It has actually been proposed—even, I am sorry to say, by two of my successors at the Office of White House Counsel—that a president could pardon himself. This, too, is a "vacancy" sign of the times. Not only is self-pardon ethically ridiculous, it is legally absurd as a construction of the Constitution. Let us see why.

In the first place, the constitutional text employs the term "grant" to denote the power exercised by the president. A grant is a conveyance or act by which a chattel or status—some good—is generally taken from one party and given to another. A president cannot, any more than anyone else, be both grantor and grantee of precisely the same thing. As a matter of original intent, the concept of a pardon power was borrowed by the Framers from the British monarchy, which over many centuries held it to be an act of clemency, a Christian act of forgiveness that one can hardly award to oneself. (I am indebted to the constitutional scholar Akhil Amar for the Zeno-esque observation that if the grant of a pardon for illicit purposes can be a crime, then a president who pardons himself must then issue another pardon to insulate that pardon, and another one to protect him from prosecution for that pardon, and so on infinitely.)

Moreover, as a matter of the American constitutional ethos, we have a long-standing principle, applying not only to reprieves and pardons but to prosecutions, judgments, and even jury participation, that no one can be a judge in his own cause. This is captured by the familiar legal phrase "*nemo judex in causa sua.*"

Nor should it be dismissed that giving the president the power of self-pardon effectively licenses him to commit any crime with impunity, subject only to impeachment which he might then by illegal means—including the arrest and detention of members of Congress—evade.

Furthermore, at the Convention Edmund Randolph made the proposal that treason be exempted from the scope of the pardon power. "The President may himself be guilty. . . . The Traytors may be his own instruments." In response to this concern, James Wilson replied that were the president "himself a party to the guilt, he can be impeached and prosecuted." With this assurance, Randolph's concern was set aside and no exemption for treason was made to the pardon power of the president. Obviously, a self-pardon is inconsistent with this colloquy.

Finally, we have the Nixon precedent. Had Nixon been able to pardon himself, there was little reason for him not to do so, thereby sparing Ford the political cost of pardoning him and avoiding the possibility that Ford would decline to do it (as President George W. Bush declined to pardon a White House subordinate of his).

Putting aside, however, the moral opprobrium that would cling to such an action, there is cause for circumspection on the part of the president regardless of his sensitivities. A self-pardon, like any other pardon, might imply to the public that a crime has been committed, a concession the president might not wish to make if he has any doubts about the validity of his reprieve.

Nor are pardons entirely beneficial for a White House hoping to free itself of an entangling investigation. Once potential witnesses are pardoned, they may no longer claim Fifth Amendment immunity when testifying before Congressional tribunals, because they are already immunized from prosecution. Here, the road to presidential impeachment may lie directly through his pardon of others, who in addition to losing some shields of due process may also lose their incentive to protect him.

It remains only to observe that for the president to grant a pardon to a potential witness in order to protect himself in such circumstances would itself be an impeachable offense. It would constitute a bribe and a patent refusal to see that the duties of the chief law enforcement officer have been faithfully executed.

Incitement

It is an open question—but not one that we lack the methods to answer—whether incitements to violence against protestors, the news media, ethnic or religious groups, or members of the bureaucracy and the judiciary amount to "high Crimes and Misdemeanors." I suppose it would depend on the consistency and persistence of the incitements, the practical effects on the body politic of such septic exhortations, and even the seriousness with which they are made (and taken). Such a fact-centered inquiry is analogous to the investigation of a president's motives to determine whether he has committed bribery. In both cases, the same acts might or might not serve as a valid predicate for impeachment, depending on context and circumstances. It would be primarily a prudential constitutional inquiry, examining the practical effects of such incitements and whether they put the country at risk of civil conflict. We have never had to confront such a possibility, but the increasing vituperation of public life and the lack of scruple with which accusations are made from many quarters can create an atmosphere in which a president who both contributes to and benefits politically from this debased condition might be removed from office after a historic tragedy.

Intimidation

For nearly a year in 1988, the Speaker of the House, Jim Wright, was the subject of philippics by a then little-known congressman from Georgia, Newt Gingrich, who called Wright, among other things, "a crook." The House Ethics Committee subsequently asserted that it found numerous examples of Wright's having accepted personal gifts and of a possible evasion of limits on outside income through a publishing arrangement, and it made other accusations, all of which Wright denied. The Democratic caucus was shaken, however, by Gingrich's vituperative charges and sought to replace Wright with a more avuncular member, Thomas Foley, who it was thought might be less of a lightning rod for criticism going into the midterm elections. In a floor speech on April 30, 1989, that ended with his dramatic resignation, Wright called for an end to the "mindless cannibalism" and the "manic idea of a frenzy of feeding on other people's reputations." By the time Gingrich himself was ejected from the speakership by his caucus—and had been the subject of far more serious ethics charges than Wright—the permissible grounds of political attack among officeholders had changed. It didn't help that the impeachment of Bill Clinton—led by Speaker Gingrich—arose from an embarrassing sexual affair, revealing a character blemish that, it turned out, was shared by the Speaker, his successor as Speaker, *his* successor as Speaker, the chief House manager of the impeachment, and other House members who had voted to impeach Clinton.

If impeachment was the catalyst for this deplorable loss of decorum, it was also a consequence. Should we now expect the impeachment process to have further consequences? That is, should we be alert to changes in the president's behavior that mirror these developments in Congress? Claims of criminal wrongdoing are far less significant when made by a House committee or a member than when they are made by an executive with the power to prosecute. What if the president directed the Department of Justice to initiate investigations to punish or disgrace his political adversaries?

Throughout 2017 the president repeatedly claimed that serious crimes had been committed by the Democratic nominee for the presidency in 2016; by the director of the FBI; by the former director of the CIA; by the former director for National Intelligence; by the ranking Democratic member of the House Intelligence Committee; by the ranking member of the Senate Intelligence Committee; by the former chairman of the Senate Intelligence Committee; by the former attorney general; and, perhaps most egregiously, by his predecessor, the former president, who he claimed had illegally wiretapped him.

If a president followed up such political rhetoric by initiating actual prosecutions of charges he knew or should have known to be baseless, there might well be grounds that he had abused his powers as the chief law enforcement officer to such a degree that he had committed a "high Crime."

Emoluments

It ought to be obvious that not every violation of a duty or prohibition whatsoever specified by the Constitution is necessarily an impeachable offense. If the president garbles the words of the Oath of Office, he can scarcely be impeached for it, although the duty is specific and unqualified. Suppose, then, that a president with a worldwide commercial enterprise based on the marketing of his surname as a brand refused to cease his involvement with this enterprise on entering office. Does the recognition and protection of his trademarks by foreign governments constitute an "emolument" forbidden by Article II? Suppose this global enterprise also sells and rents residential and commercial real estate, and that foreign governments or their corrupt allies in authoritarian states surge to buy these properties when the new president is inaugurated. Does his retention of his interests, however passive, amount to a prohibited emolument?

The attitude of the Framers and ratifiers can be gleaned from American reaction to the XYZ Affair, which precipitated the first international war of the United States. The affair embarrassed the Adams administration, which had sought diplomatic negotiations with France only to be rebuffed until payments were made to the French foreign minister, Talleyrand. This was a common European practice at the time, although Talleyrand seems to have exceeded even the capacious moral boundaries of the age; he was known to receive a vast retainer from the czar even during periods of Franco-Russian conflict. One of his methods of earning income was to sell or rent châteaux to government officials, who felt obliged to comply.

The application of the Emoluments Clause to the president has been disputed on textual grounds. It is said that the president does not hold an "Office . . . under the United States" because the presidency is created by Article II of the Constitution and not by the Congress, whereas other parts of the Constitution that employ this phrase do not refer to constitutionally created offices. Recent precedent—President Obama's receipt of the Nobel Prize, for example—goes the other way and requires divestiture.

For our purposes, the issue is slightly different: Even assuming that a president's refusal to divest himself of profitable commercial ventures that are engaged with foreign governments is inconsistent with the Emoluments Clause, is it a valid ground for impeachment? That is, is it a constitutional crime that strikes at the stability and viability of the State? *Federalist* #73 seems to advise a complete disposition of any problematic assets. The purpose of the Emoluments Clause, we are told, is to ensure that the president "can have no pecuniary inducement to renounce or desert the independence intended for him by the Constitution." It seems that we are left to decide whether the president's financial interests abroad—or their entanglement with foreign interests at home—truly jeopardize the integrity of the United States. This is a fact-based inquiry by the Senate, the constitutionally designated trier of fact in impeachments.

Perhaps the recent interest in the Emoluments Clause is not, however, merely an artifact of having a wealthy commercial promoter and businessman in high office but arises instead from a growing concern about the commodification of politics and its effects on the legitimacy of government. That these doubts have been stoked by the businessman's campaign—charging that the system is "rigged," that millions of votes were cast illegally, that his opponent should be sent to prison, and so forth—may simply be an example of the old football adage that the "best defense is a good offense." In any case, the unease that pervades the current assessment of our institutions and their vitality is not going away.

We are moving, I believe, from the sort of State we have had since the Civil War—and a constitutional order that we share with other states that is committed to enforcing the values and improving the welfare of the dominant national group through law and the regulation of the market—to an informational state that prefers to use the market when it can, in preference to law, in order to maximize the wealth of society and the opportunities of individuals. That we should have harvested an entrepreneurial leader with no commitment to the political status quo—or to customary legal practices, for that matter—should not surprise us. Our task will be to harmonize these historic developments with the commitments of the Constitution, and that task cannot begin with simply rejecting what will seem to many to be very unsettling events.

Incapacitation: The Twenty-Fifth Amendment

The same forces that have brought an entrepreneurial leader to the White House are reflected in many other changes in the American constitutional order. Industrial nation-states used law and regulation to tame the market. State-owned enterprises abounded: airlines, energy companies, transportation networks, telecoms. Most industrial nation-states had a national health service and a system of public universities with modest student fees. Banks were heavily regulated, and in many countries the same organization could not conduct both depositary and investment operations. The price of gold and the relative values of currencies were negotiated by states. The international movement of capital was strictly controlled.

With the end of the Cold War and the development of technologies that empowered globalization, all that began to change, and a new, insurgent constitutional order began to emerge. This new constitutional order—the informational market-state—relied on the market rather than attempting to control it and steadily abandoned the industrial nation-state's legal enforcement of the dominant national group's moral commitments. The legitimacy of the informational market-state was based on the premise that success in the postwar world would accrue to the state that maximized its society's total wealth by providing sustained economic growth, and that the way to do that was to increase the opportunities for all citizens. New policies and practices began to appear as harbingers of this new constitutional order.

When states go from a reliance on law and regulation, so characteristic of the industrial nation-state, to deregulation not only of industries but, far more importantly, of women's reproduction; when they move from armies raised by conscription to an all-volunteer force, as all the most powerful states have done; when they end their policies of tuition-free higher education in favor of tuition fees and need-based and merit-based scholarships; when they go from providing direct cash transfers like unemployment compensation to job-skills training to get workers back into the labor market; when state-owned enterprises are replaced by sovereign wealth funds; when market-based regimes of direct democracy like referenda, recall votes, political polling, and voter initiatives begin to spread in preference to representational systems, turning citizens of a polity into consumers of its political products—when all this happens, we are seeing the beginnings of a change in the constitutional order.

One such change may be the adaptation of the Twenty-Fifth Amendment as a supplement to impeachment, triggering action in Congress, rather like voter initiatives that can propose statutes and thus prompt legislative action.

The Twenty-Fifth Amendment was a direct consequence of the assassination of President John F. Kennedy. After the disputed succession of John Tyler, it had been accepted that a vice-president would accede to the office of the presidency on the death or removal from office of the president. But what if Kennedy had lived in an incapacitated state, as James Garfield did for almost three months? Or what if Lyndon Johnson, who had had a near fatal heart attack in 1955, was felled by a debilitating but not fatal stroke, like the one that left Woodrow Wilson an invalid for the last eighteen months of his term? These questions were addressed by the Twenty-Fifth Amendment, which provides, among other things, that if the vice-president and a majority of the cabinet (or such other body as Congress may designate) inform the Senate and House that the president is "unable to discharge the power and duties of his office," the vice-president shall immediately assume those authorities. If the president disputes this action, Congress shall decide, by a two-thirds vote of both Houses, whether the vice-president shall continue as acting president or the president shall resume his powers.

Although the intention behind the Amendment was clearly to address physical disabilities, its language is not so limited. Unlike impeachment, the grounds for removal are not specified. It may be that some future president will be removed when two-thirds of the Congress wish to do so on grounds of maladministration or even over policy differences. This would be a large step toward a parliamentary government, because the Senate can control the membership of the cabinet, and in any event, the Congress can designate the group that along with the vice-president—who is hardly a disinterested party—is charged with certifying the president's inability to govern.

It does not matter that such a revolutionary change is incompatible with the plan of the Framers and ratifiers of the unamended text; it's the intentions of the Framers and ratifiers of the Amendment and the text of that Amendment that count. The check on such an alteration in our constitutional plan might then lie with the judiciary, which could affirm or deny an extraordinary writ brought to determine the identity of the lawful occupant of the presidential office.

All this lies pregnant in our Constitution; let us hope it has a long gestation period.

CHAPTER 9

Decision according to Law

Is the decision to impeach and then to convict the president a matter of law?

The first question must be: Are we bound by the legal interpretation of the Constitution on any subject that has not been, and may never be, adjudicated by the US Supreme Court? If the answer is no, doesn't this simply amount to "might makes right," the ancient notion that whoever has the ultimate power to make a decision is *ipso facto* correct as to the law? On this view, sovereignty simply lies with the effective decider. If that is true, then it would seem to apply to the Supreme Court as well, whose decisions are, after all, not reviewable. But then why do our various deciders bother with judicial opinions, presidential statements, congressional resolutions, rules, or precedents?

There are those who do not shrink from such conclusions; like most cynics, they call themselves "realists." But is their account an accurate description of the way things really operate in the American constitutional system? (It's interesting that the persons who make such claims rarely have experience in government service.) Is the Supreme Court—or the Congress, with respect to impeachment—infallible *because* it is final? If not, if other branches and our people must concur and accept the decisions of government, then perhaps such decisions are not as final as they seem. If *that* is the case, how do they—and we—determine what is right when the mighty disagree, or fumble for reasons to account for their actions?

The whole theory of American government, limned in the Declaration of Independence and given operational form in the Constitution, is that power alone does not legitimate, that legitimacy can only come from the adherence to the rule of law by means of which our People have accorded power to government. This theory will always be tested. Each generation will live out the experiments that verify or falsify it. It may ultimately prove a tragedy, but it is not farce or a charade—not yet, anyway.

Are there neutral, general principles for all constitutional questions? If there are, why should they guide us? And if they should, how would that guidance work? If after a conscientious attempt to discern and apply the law, we disagreed and found the law insufficiently determinate to compel a consensus, how would we resolve that conflict? Why wouldn't such an impasse show that the whole enterprise was a waste of time—or worse, a mystifying facade?

We begin by insisting that we really are trying to be neutral, general, and principled in applying the rules we can agree on. With respect to impeachment, we must imagine that the president to be impeached is of the opposite party to the one being tried. If we think the Emoluments Clause forbids substantial income to the incumbent of the White House outside his salary, we must ask ourselves whether we would also have required the Clinton Foundation to dissolve itself in order to avoid the appearance of transgression. We must imagine that a similar case could come up in the future for which the impeachment today would serve as a controlling precedent. If we say that a president cannot be impeached for actions he took while a candidate, we must be willing to apply that rule to candidates we admire as much as to those we dislike. We must be able to state a clear and coherent principle. An example might be *Actions taken before holding office cannot serve as the grounds for the impeachment of a president unless they bear on the electoral process itself.* Is that statement sufficiently robust to be applied by other deciders than ourselves? What does "bear on the electoral process" mean?

Thus we test our fidelity to the rule of law by imagining whether we would be willing and able, in the case of crafting a workable principle, to apply rules to presidents toward whom we might feel differently than we do toward the incumbent.

How do we derive these principles? We begin with the six fundamental forms of argument, which can be found just as clearly in *McCulloch* v. *Maryland* as in Charles Black's *Handbook*: history, text, structure, doctrine, prudence and ethos. But that doesn't end the matter, nor should it. Our system of government presumes that the individual conscience will play a decisive role, whether it is the conscience of the member of Congress trying a case of impeachment, a juror trying a civil or criminal matter, or an appellate judge drafting an opinion. We cannot preclude the role of the individual decision maker, nor should we want to. To see this necessity as a flaw is to miss the historic character and meaning of our system, which structures our decisions according to legal argumentation but ultimately requires a conscientious choice by the decider once those structures have done their work.

So we are compelled to ask: What weight do we give to previous impeachments? How do we complete the series "treason, bribery, [and other such offenses]"? What weight should we give the removal from office of executives of the state governments before the Constitution was ratified? What are the implications for impeachment of the Framers' and ratifiers' rejection of the parliamentary practice of the vote of no-confidence? Do we actually wish to divert executive resources through constant investigation and harrying of executive officials? What weight should we give the texts of the crucial

Civil War amendments in construing the earlier provisions those amendments were meant to modify? And what of the intentions of the framers and ratifiers of those amendments? What weight should we give statements at the Constitutional Convention relative to the statements in the *Federalist Papers* regarding impeachment? Does it matter that the language of the grounds for impeachment is the same for members of the executive as well as the judiciary? How should we understand earlier presidents' actions during times of crisis—Jefferson's purchase of Louisiana without an appropriation from Congress, Lincoln's suspension of habeas corpus, FDR's warrantless interception of international communications during World War II—that might otherwise be grounds for impeachment? What rules do we want to craft now that can be applied in future instances of presidential misbehavior (or can deter such misbehavior)?

Suppose that, in all good conscience, we still disagree. Does that mean that impeachment isn't a matter of law? That our attempts to craft a constitutional rule amount to no more than, as one law professor put it, constitutional "fetishism"?

It's a good thing that our attention is drawn to these questions, because otherwise we might be inclined to forget the answers. It in fact reflects the insight and wisdom of our Framers and ratifiers that in the most difficult cases, the rule of law in America is made to depend on our individual consciences. These difficult cases are rarer than the skeptic would have us believe, but they are just as important as he claims. Rather than growing dispirited, however, we should feel inspired. That's what the legal term "inalienable" requires: that the most consequential decisions are ultimately up to us and can't be delegated.

The most important contribution of *Impeachment: A Handbook* was to insist on the legal nature of the indictment and trial of the president by the Congress, and to show how this should be done according to law even though there were no authoritative judicial precedents. This perspective has many implications for partisanship and for citizenship. It bears on issues of executive privilege, the office of an independent counsel, and many other questions collateral to impeachment itself.

*

> Out of the turbulence of the sea,
> Flower by brittle flower, rises
> The coral reef that calms the water

> —Archibald MacLeish

The architects that preceded us in ceaseless labor, life after life, built on the inherited acropolis of law a constitutional structure ever-changing, ever-enduring, unfinished, in parts neglected and decaying, obdurate yet imagined. Their legacy resides in the methods by which, case by case, generation by generation, the barriers of law channel the tumults of politics and power toward justice and equality, and away from violence and cruel oppression. Their genius was to deliver to us a temple whose innermost chamber contains a question. They could not decide for us, but they could give us the ways our decisions are assessed and explained. Having mastered the ways of the law that they taught us, we must in the end find our own answers to the awesome questions that mastery poses but cannot resolve.

Someday, if we're lucky, our descendants will struggle as we do with such decisions. Will they make them according to law or will they sell, or barter, or give them away to those who are only too happy to decide without having to explain?

I, for one, am an optimist. That, you may recall, is how we began—how I began these chapters, how we began this country.

Appendix

The following are the provisions in the Constitution most relevant to the subject of this book, with emphasis added:

ARTICLE I

. . . .

Section 2. . . . .

[5] The House of Representatives shall chuse their Speaker and other Officers; *and shall have the sole Power of Impeachment.*

Section 3. . . . .

[6] *The Senate shall have the sole Power to try all Impeachments. When sitting for that Purpose, they shall be on Oath or Affirmation.* When the President of the United States is tried, the Chief Justice shall preside: And no Person shall be convicted without the Concurrence of two thirds of the Members present.

[7] Judgment in Cases of Impeachment shall not extend further than to removal from Office, and disqualification to hold and enjoy any Office of honor, Trust, or Profit under the United States: but the Party convicted shall nevertheless be liable and subject to Indictment, Trial, Judgment, and Punishment, according to Law.

. . . .

Section 9. . . . .

[3] No Bill of Attainder or ex post facto Law shall be passed.

. . . .

Section 10 [1] No State shall enter into any Treaty, Alliance, or Confederation; grant Letters of Marque and Reprisal; coin Money; emit Bills of Credit; make any Thing but gold and silver Coin a Tender in Payment of Debts; *pass any Bill of Attainder, ex post facto Law,* or Law impairing the Obligations of Contracts, or grant any Title of Nobility.

. . . .

[8] No Title of Nobility shall be granted by the United States; And no Person holding any Office of Profit or Trust under them, shall, without the Consent of Congress, *accept any present, Emolument, Office, or Title, of any kind whatever, from any King, Prince, or foreign State.*

. . . .

ARTICLE II

Section 1. . . . .

[8] Before he enter on the Execution of his Office, he shall take the following Oath or Affirmation: "I do solemnly swear (or affirm) that I will faithfully execute the Office of President of the United States, and will to the best of my Ability, preserve, protect and defend the Constitution of the United States."

Section 2 [1]. . . . .

he shall have Power to grant Reprieves and Pardons for Offenses against the United States, except in Cases of Impeachment.

. . . .

Section 3 He shall from time to time give to the Congress Information of the State of the Union, and recommend to their Consideration such Measures as he shall judge necessary and expedient; he may, on the extraordinary Occasions, convene both Houses, or either of them, and in Case of Disagreement between them, with Respect to the Time of Adjournment, he may adjourn them to such Time as he shall think proper; he shall receive Ambassadors and other public Ministers; *he shall take Care that the Laws be faithfully executed,* and shall Commission all the officers of the United States.

Section 4 The President, Vice President and all civil Officers of the United States, *shall be removed from Office on Impeachment for, and Conviction of, Treason, Bribery, or other high Crimes and Misdemeanors.*

ARTICLE III

Section 1 The Judicial Power of the United States, shall be vested in one supreme Court, and in such inferior Courts as the Congress may from time to time ordain and establish. The Judges, both of the supreme and inferior Courts, shall hold their Offices during good Behaviour, and shall, at stated Times, receive for their Services a Compensation, which shall not be diminished during their Continuance in Office.

Section 2 [1] *The judicial Power shall extend to all Cases, in Law and Equity, arising under this Constitution, the Laws of the United States, and Treaties made, or which shall be made, under their Authority;*—to all Cases affecting Ambassadors, other public Ministers and Consuls;—to all Cases of admiralty and maritime Jurisdiction;—to Controversies to which the United States shall be a Party;—to Controversies between two or more States;—between a State and Citizens of another State;—between Citizens of different States;—between Citizens of the same State claiming Lands under the Grants of different States, and between a State, or the Citizens thereof, and foreign States, Citizens or Subjects.

[2] In all Cases affecting Ambassadors, other public Ministers and Consuls, and those in which a State shall be a Party, the supreme Court shall have original Jurisdiction. In all the other Cases before mentioned, the supreme Court shall have appellate Jurisdiction, both as to Law and Fact, *with such Exceptions, and under such Regulations as the Congress shall make.*

[3] The trial of all Crimes, except in Cases of Impeachment, shall be by Jury; and such Trial shall be held in the State where the said Crimes shall have been committed; but when not committed within any State, the Trial shall be at such Place or Places as the Congress may by Law have directed.

Section 3 [1] *Treason against the United States, shall consist only in levy-ing War against them, or, in adhering to their Enemies, giving them Aid and Comfort.* No Person shall be convicted of Treason unless on the Testimony of two Witnesses to the same overt Act, or on Confession in open Court.

AMENDMENT XXV

. . . .

Section 4 Whenever the Vice President and a majority of either the principal officers of the executive departments or of such other body as Congress may by law provide, transmit to the President pro tempore of the Senate and the Speaker of the House of Representatives their written declaration that the President is unable to discharge the powers and duties of his office, the Vice President shall immediately assume the powers and duties of the office as Acting President. Thereafter when the President transmits to the President pro tempore of the Senate and the Speaker of the House of Representatives his written declaration that no inability exists, he shall resume the powers and duties of his office unless the Vice President and a majority of either the principal officers of the executive department or of such other body as Congress may by law provide, transmit within four days to the President pro tempore of the Senate and the Speaker of the House of Representatives their written declaration that the President is unable to discharge the powers and duties of his office. Thereupon Congress shall decide the issue, assembling within forty-eight hours for that purpose if not in session. If the Congress, within twenty-one days after receipt of the latter written declaration, or, if Congress is not in session, within twenty-one days after Congress is required to assemble, determines by two-thirds vote of both Houses that the President is unable to discharge the powers and duties of his office, the Vice President shall continue to discharge the same as Acting President; otherwise, the President shall resume the powers and duties of his office.

Bibliography

The literature on impeachment is vast and, not surprisingly, of varying quality. Some of the most useful texts are collected below. The bibliography from the 1974 edition was reprinted from the House Judiciary Committee Staff Report on Constitutional Grounds for Presidential Impeachment, 93rd Congress, 2d Session.

Ackerman, Bruce A., *We the People* (2 vols, 1991).

Adams, Henry, *History of the United States of America during the First Administration of Thomas Jefferson* (1898).

Amar, Akhil Reed, *America's Constitution: A Biography* (2006).

Amar, Akhil Reed, "On Impeaching Presidents," 28 *Hofstra L. R.* 291 (1999).

Association of the Bar of the City of New York, *The Law of Presidential Impeachment and Removal* (1974).

Balkin, Jack, and Sanford Levinson, *Legal Canons* (2000).

Barr, Bob, "High Crimes and Misdemeanors: The Clinton-Gore Scandals and the Question of Impeachment," 2 *Tex. Rev. L. & Pol'y* 1 (1997).

Bartrum, Ian C., "The Modalities of Constitutional Argument: A Primer," *Readings in Persuasion: Briefs That Changed the World*, ed. Linda Edwards (2011), https://papers.ssrn.com/sol3/papers.cfm?abstract_id=1849263.

Berger, Raoul, *Impeachment: The Constitutional Problems* (1973).

Black, Charles, "A Note on Senatorial Consideration of Supreme Court Nominees," (1970), http://digitalcommons.law.yale.edu/cgi/view content.cgi?article=3583&context=fss_papers.

Bobbitt, Philip, *Constitutional Interpretation* (1991).

Brant, Irving, *Impeachment: Trials and Errors* (1972).

Bryce, James, *The American Commonwealth* (1931).

Calabresi, Massimo, "Inside Russia's Social Media War on America," *TIME*, May 18, 2017.

Chafetz, Josh, *Congress's Constitution: Legislative Authority and the Separation of Powers* (2017).

Clinton v. *Jones*, 520 U.S. 681 (1998).

Congressional Research Service on Grounds for Impeachment, https://llb2.com/2017/08/30/congressional-research-service-on-grounds-for-impeachment-resources/ (2017).

"Constitutional Grounds for Presidential Impeachment," Report by the Staff of the Impeachment Inquiry, Committee on the Judiciary, House of Representatives, 93rd Congress, 2nd session (1974).

Cutler, Lloyd, "To Form a Government," *Foreign Affairs*, Fall 1980.

Davidson, Roger, "Congress after 1994: Political Tides and Institutional Change," 13 *Brookings Rev.* 26 (1995).

Dewitt, David M., *The Impeachment and Trial of Andrew Johnson, Seventeenth President of the United States: A History* (1967).

Dwight, Theodore, "Trial by Impeachment," 6 *Am. L. Reg. (N.S.)* 257 (1867).

Elliot, Jonathan, *The Debates in the Several State Conventions on the Adoption of the Federal Constitution* (2d ed., 1827).

Ethridge, George, "The Law of Impeachment," 8 *Miss. L. J.* 283 (1936).

Fallon, Richard H., Jr., "A Constructivist Coherence Theory of Constitutional Interpretation," 100 *Harv. L. Rev.* 1189 (1987).

Farrand, Max, *The Records of the Federal Convention of 1787* (1937).

Feerick, John, "Impeaching Federal Judges: A Study of the Constitutional Provisions," 30 *Fordham L. Rev.* 1 (1970).

Fenton, Paul, "The Scope of the Impeachment Power," 65 *NW. U. L. Rev.* 719 (1970).

Finley, John, and John Sanderson, *The American Executive and Executive Methods* (1908).

Gerhardt, Michael J., *The Federal Impeachment Process: A Constitutional and Historical Analysis* (1996).

Hamilton, Alexander, James Madison, and John Jay, *The Federalist*, ed., with Introduction and Historical Commentary by J. R. Pole (2005).

Hinds, Asher C., *Hinds' Precedents of the House of Representatives of the United States: Including References to Provisions of the Constitution, the Laws, and Decisions of the United States Senate*, 59th Congress, 2d Session (1907), http://www.gpo.gov/congress/house/precedents/hinds/hinds.html.

House Document 105-311, "Communication from the Office of the Independent Counsel, Kenneth W. Starr," September 9, 1998. Accessed via https://www.gpo.gov/fdsys/pkg/GPO-CDOC-105hdoc311/content-detail.html.

Isenbergh, Joseph, *Impeachment and Presidential Immunity from Judicial Process* (1998).

Jefferson, Thomas, *Jefferson's Manual of Parliamentary Practice* (1801), reprinted in *Constitution, Jefferson's Manual, and Rules of the House of Representatives of the United States, H.R. Doc. No. 104-272* (1997).

Jordan, Barbara, "Testimony before the House Judiciary Committee," 5 *Tex. J. Women & the Law* 161 (1996).

Kadish, Sanford H., Stephen J. Schulhofer, and Rachel E. Barkow, *Criminal Law and Its Processes* (10th ed., 2017).

Kalt, Brian C., "Pardon Me? The Constitutional Case Against Presidential Self-Pardons," 106 *Yale L. J.* 779 (1996).

Katyal, Neal, *Impeachment as Congressional Constitutional Interpretation* (2000).

Klarman, Michael J., "Constitutional Fetishism and the Clinton Impeachment Debate," 85 *Va. L. Rev.* 631 (1999).

Labovitz, John, *Presidential Impeachment* (1978).

Lawrence, William, "A Brief of the Authorities upon the Law of Impeachable Crimes and Misdemeanors," *Congressional Globe Supplement*, 40th Congress, 2d Session, at 41 (1868).

Levinson, Sanford, "Constitutional Protestantism in Theory and Practice: Two Questions for Michael Stokes Paulsen and One for His Critics," 83 *Geo. L.J. 373* (1994).

Library of Congress, *Impeachment,* https://www.loc.gov/law/find/impeachment.php (2002).

Library of Congress, *Supplement to the Congressional Globe Containing the Proceedings of the Senate Sitting for the Trial of Andrew Johnson,* http://memory.loc.gov/ammem/amlaw/lwcg-imp.html.

Linde, Hans A., "Replacing a President: RX for a 21st Century Watergate," 43 *Geo. Wash. L. Rev.* 384 (1975).

Lipton, Eric, David Sanger, and Scott Shane, "The Perfect Weapon: How Russia Invaded the U.S.," *New York Times,* Dec. 13, 2016.

Mann, Thomas, and Norman Ornstein, *It's Even Worse Than It Was: How the American Constitutional System Collided with the New Politics of Extremism* (2016).

Morgan, Edmund S., *Inventing the People: The Rise of Popular Sovereignty in England and America* (1988).

Nixon v. *United States,* 506 U.S. 224 (1993).

Note, "The Exclusiveness of the Impeachment Power under the Constitution," 51 *Harv. L. Rev.* 330 (1937).

Ogden, David W., Deputy Attorney General, "Memorandum for Selected United States Attorneys" (2009), https://www.justice.gov/archives/opa/blog/memorandum-selected-united-state-attorneys-investigations-and-prosecutions-states.

Pious, Richard M., "Impeaching the President: The Intersection of Constitutional and Popular Law," 43 *St. Louis U. L. J.* 859 (1999).

Posner, Richard A., *An Affair of State: The Investigation, Impeachment, and Trial of President Clinton* (1999).

Powell, H. Jefferson, "The Original Understanding of Original Intent," 98 *Harv. L. Rev.* 885 (1985).

Powell, H. Jefferson, *The President as Commander in Chief* (2014).

Radnofsky, Barbara, *A Citizen's Guide to Impeachment* (2017).

Rakove, Jack, "Statement on the Background and History of Impeachment," 67 *Geo. Wash. L. Rev.* 682 (1999).

Rawle, William, *A View of the Constitution of the United States* (2 vol. ed., 1829).

Rehnquist, William H., *Grand Inquests: The Historic Impeachments of Justice Samuel Chase and President Andrew Johnson* (1999).

"Rules of Procedure and Practice in the Senate when Sitting on Impeachment Trials," Senate Manual, S. Doc. 113th Congress (2014).

Sachs, Richard, *Role of Vice-President Designate Gerald Ford in the Attempt to Impeach Associate Supreme Court Justice William O. Douglas*, Legislative Reference Service (1973). Accessed via Gerald R. Ford Library.

Scalia, Antonin, *A Matter of Interpretation: Federal Courts and the Law* (1997).

Story, Joseph, *Commentaries on the Constitution of the United States* (5th edition, 1801).

Sunstein, Cass R., *Impeachment: A Citizen's Guide* (2017).

Symposium, "The American Constitutional Tradition of Shared and Separated Powers," 30 *Wm. & Mary L. Rev.* 209 (1989).

Thomas, David, "The Law of Impeachment in the United States," 2 *Am. Pol. Sci. Rev.* 378 (1908).

Tillman, Seth Barrett, and Steven Calabresi, "The Great Divorce: The Current Understanding of Separation of Powers and the Original Meaning of the Incompatibility Clause," 157 *U. Pa. L. Rev.* 134 (2008).

Tribe, Laurence, and Joshua Matz, *To End a Presidency: The Power of Impeachment* (2018).

Tushnet, Mark, *Evaluating Congressional Constitutional Interpretation: Some Criteria and Two Informal Case Studies* (2001).

US Senate, "Report of the Congressional Committees Investigating the Iran-Contra Affair: With Supplemental, Minority, and Additional Views," S. Rpt. No. 100-216 (1987).

The text of *Impeachment: A Handbook* is not annotated, in keeping with the practice of the original edition. The material added for the present edition, however, includes a good deal of historical information and relies on legal materials beyond the text, history, and structure of the Constitution. For this reason, the *Yale Law Journal* has published, roughly contemporaneously with this edition of *Impeachment*, an article composed of the new chapters with extensive footnotes.

Acknowledgments

My thanks are owed to Barbara Black for approving this project and to William Frucht for supervising it, editing my chapters, and—with Ann-Marie Imbornoni—bringing it to life.

Once again, my incomparable secretary, Ms. Jennifer Lamar—with the additional distraction of two young children of her own—has patiently and thoughtfully brought a manuscript of mine through many versions into publication.

Research assistance was given me by Andrew Elliott, Philippe Schiff, Yasmine Smith, Jaclyn Willner, and Andrew Connery. The true depth of their help will be apparent when readers consult my text accompanied by notes. I am grateful to the *Yale Law Journal*, and to its editor in chief, Chloe Jacoby, for arranging the publication of that text with extensive footnotes in the *Journal*, to be published contemporaneously with the present work in order to provide a resource for students, scholars, lawyers, and public officials who wish to master the raw materials behind the arguments.

The poets David Ferry, Betty Sue Flowers, and Robert Pinsky gave me helpful and inspiriting comments as I endeavored to write a commentary for a general audience.

My greatest debt, of course, is owed to the original genius of the first edition, Charles L. Black, Jr. As I have so often, I wish he were here. I would like to inscribe a copy of the new edition: "For Charles: You entrusted these ideas to us once. Now I pass that trust on to others."

I am ever aware when I write anything in constitutional law of my debts to Akhil Amar. Twenty-five years ago, he claimed to be my student; he later became my teacher. As Charles Black once wrote me, "You taught me it is never too late to make an old friend."

For everything else, I rely on Maya Ondalikoglu Bobbitt, without whom little else would matter.

Impeachment is a terrible, awesome subject, fraught with all the risks that accompany major surgery to the body politic, sounded in somber tones that recall historic regicides, muted by the methods of law. Should our country have need of this book again, I count on it being read with solemnity and dread, and, if necessary, applied with resolution and courage.

Index

Adams, John, 112
Adams, John Quincy, 99, 103, 139
Amar, Akhil, 101, 135, 155

Barr, Bob, 155
Berger, Raoul, 155
bill of attainder, 26, 28–30, 106
Black, Charles L., Jr., xi–xii, 65–66, 82,
    87, 95, 105, 108–109, 111–112, 117,
    121, 129, 131, 134, 147, 156, 161–162
Blackstone's *Commentaries on the Law
    of England*, 101
bribery, 15, 25–28, 30, 32, 34–35, 37, 38,
    41, 94, 101, 109–110, 131–132, 134,
    137, 147, 152
    Impeachment Clause, 3, 13–14,
        24–26, 35, 37, 101, 106, 110, 131, 152
    See also emoluments
British impeachment, 118
burglary, xi, 67–68, 124–125
    cyberburglary (hacking), xi, 122,
        124, 126
Burr, Aaron, 110–111
Bush, George W., 65, 83–84, 136

campaign tactics, improper, 40–41
censure, 17, 60
Central Intelligence Agency (CIA),
    69–70, 72, 75, 115, 138

Chase, Samuel, 103, 110
Chennault, Anna, 91–92
chief justice, role in impeachment,
    11–13, 48, 103, 151
Chong, Jane, 102
Clinton, Bill
    House impeachment of, xii, 65–66,
        75–83, 90, 102, 108, 120, 138
    independent counsel investigation,
        77–80
    Senate acquittal, 65, 83, 100, 102
    Whitewater controversy, 75–78
Clinton v. Jones, 156
collusion, 92, 94, 130
Committee of Twelve, 13
Constitutional Convention, 11, 25–26,
    50, 52, 90, 100, 148
constitutional interpretation. *See* forms
    of constitutional argument
constitutional order, 86, 120, 141–143
corruption, 16–17, 93, 117, 124
criminal acts, 36, 97, 107, 109

Declaration of Independence, 146
Development, Relief and Education for
    Alien Minors Act (DREAM Act), 87
Dirksen, Everett, 92
discretionary duties, impeachment for,
    38, 86–89, 97–98, 113–116